THE ROMAN PONTIFICAL
Revised by Decree of the Second Vatican Ecumenical Council
and Published by Authority of Pope Paul VI

DEDICATION OF A CHURCH AND AN ALTAR

Provisional Text

Copublished by Catholic Truth Society, London; Veritas Publications, Dublin;
United States Conference of Catholic Bishops, Washington, D.C.

Revised 1989

English Translation Prepared by the
International Commission on English in the Liturgy
A Joint Commission of Catholic Bishops' Conferences

Bishops' Committee for the Liturgy
United States Conference of Catholic Bishops
Washington, D.C.

The English translation of liturgical texts in this publication has been approved for use in the dioceses of the United States by the Bishops' Committee on the Liturgy and the Executive Committee of the National Conference of Catholic Bishops and has been confirmed *ad interim* by the Apostolic See, the Congregation for the Sacraments and Divine Worship (Prot. CD 1016/78, September 25, 1978).

✝ Joseph P. Delaney
Bishop of Fort Worth
Chairman
Bishops' Committee on the Liturgy

August 15, 1989

Concordat cum originali:
Reverend Ronald F. Krisman
Executive Director
Secretariat for the Liturgy
National Conference of Catholic Bishops
August 15, 1989

The English translation of the liturgical texts in this publication has been approved for the continued *ad interim* use by Bishops of England and Wales.

✝ Mervyn
Bishop of Clifton

February 2, 1990

This text was typeset and printed in the United States of America and, therefore, has adopted American spelling throughout.

English translation © 1978, International Committee on English in the Liturgy, Inc. (ICEL); the English translation of the Decree and the Introductions from *Documents on the Liturgy, 1963-1979: Conciliar, Papal, and Curial Texts* © 1982, ICEL; excerpts from the English translation of *Emendations in the Liturgical Books Following upon the New Code of Canon Law* © 1984, ICEL. All rights reserved.

USCCB: ISBN 1-55586-331-0
Veritas Publications: ISBN 1-85390-165-2
Catholic Truth Society: ISBN 0-86183-801-4

Also available in a paperback edition, pub. no. 283-7.

First Printing, April 1990
Second Printing, September 2001

Copyright © 1989, United States Conference of Catholic Bishops, Inc., Washington, D.C. All rights reserved. No part of this work may be reproduced or transmitted in any form or by any means, electronic or mechanical, including photocopying, recording, or by any information storage and retrieval system, without permission in writing from the copyright holder.

CONTENTS

SACRED CONGREGATION FOR THE SACRAMENTS AND DIVINE WORSHIP

Prot. no. CD 300/77

Decree

The rite for the dedication of a church and an altar is rightly considered among the most solemn liturgical services. A church is the place where the Christian community is gathered to hear the word of God, to offer intercession and praise to him, and above all to celebrate the holy mysteries, and it is the place where the holy sacrament of the eucharist is kept. Thus it stands as a special kind of image of the Church itself, which is God's temple built from living stones. And the altar of a church, around which the holy people of God gather to take part in the Lord's sacrifice and to be refreshed at the heavenly meal, stands as a sign of Christ himself, who is the priest, the victim, and the altar of his own sacrifice.

These rites, found in the second book of the Roman Pontifical, were revised and simplified in 1961. Nevertheless it was judged necessary to revise the rites again and to adapt them to contemporary conditions in view of the purpose and the norms of the liturgical reform that Vatican II set in motion and fostered.

Pope Paul VI by his authority has approved the new *Ordo dedicationis ecclesiae et altaris* prepared by the Congregation for the Sacraments and Divine Worship. He has ordered it to be published and prescribed that it replace the rites now in the second book of the Roman Pontifical.

This Congregation, by mandate of the Pope, therefore publishes this *Ordo dedicationis ecclesiae et altaris*. In the Latin text it will be in effect as soon as it appears; in the vernacular, it will take effect, after the translations have been confirmed and approved by the Apostolic See, on the day determined by the conferences of bishops.

Anything to the contrary notwithstanding.

From the office of the Congregation for the Sacraments and Divine Worship, May 29, 1977, Pentecost.

+ James R. Cardinal Knox
Prefect

+ Antonio Innocenti
Titular Archbishop of Eclano
Secretary

CHAPTER ONE

RITE OF LAYING THE FOUNDATION STONE OR BEGINNING WORK ON THE BUILDING OF A CHURCH

INTRODUCTION

1.   When the building of a new church begins, it is desirable to celebrate a rite to ask God's blessing for the success of the work and to remind the people that the structure built of stone will be a visible sign of the living Church, God's building that is formed of the people themselves.[1]

   In accordance with liturgical tradition, this rite consists of the blessing of the site of the new church and the blessing and laying of the foundation stone. When there is to be no foundation stone because of the particular architecture of the building, the rite of the blessing of the site of the new church should still be celebrated in order to dedicate the beginning of the work of God.

2.   The rite for the laying of a foundation stone or for beginning a new church may be celebrated on any day except during the Easter triduum. But the preference should be for a day when the people can be present in large numbers.

3.   The bishop of the diocese is rightly the one to celebrate the rite. If he cannot do so himself, he shall entrust the function to another bishop or a priest, especially to one who is his associate and assistant in the pastoral care of the diocese or of the community for which the new church is to be built.

4.   Notice of the date and hour of the celebration should be given to the people in good time. The pastor or others concerned should instruct them in the meaning of the rite and the reverence to be shown toward the church that is to be built for them.

   It is also desirable that the people be asked to give their generous and willing support in the building of the church.

---

[1] See 1 Cor 3:9; LG, 6.

5.   Insofar as possible, the area for the erection of the church should be marked out clearly. It should be possible to walk about without difficulty.

6.   In the place where the altar will be located, a wooden cross of suitable height is fixed in the ground.

7.   For the celebration of the rite the following should be prepared:

— The Roman Pontifical and Lectionary;

— chair for the bishop;

— depending on the circumstances, the foundation stone, which by tradition is a rectangular cornerstone, together with cement and the tools for setting the stone in the foundation;

— container of holy water with sprinkler;

— censer, incense boat and spoon;

— processional cross and torches for the servers.

Sound equipment should be set up so that the assembly can clearly hear the readings, prayers, and instructions.

8.   For the celebration of the rite the vestments are white or of some festive color. The following should be prepared:

— for the bishop: alb, stole, cope, miter, and pastoral staff;

— for the priest, when one presides over the celebration: alb, stole, and cope;

— for the deacons: albs, stoles, and if opportune, dalmatics;

— for other ministers: albs or other lawfully approved dress.

OUTLINE OF THE RITE

APPROACH TO THE CONSTRUCTION SITE
A. First Form: Procession
    Greeting
    Brief Introduction
    Prayer
    Procession

B. Second Form: Station at the Construction Site of the New Church
    Acclamation or Song
    Greeting
    Brief Instruction
    Prayer

READING OF THE WORD OF GOD
    Reading(s)
    [Responsorial Psalm]
    Homily
    Placing of the Document(s) in the Foundation Stone

BLESSING OF THE SITE OF THE NEW CHURCH
    Prayer of Blessing
    Laying of the Foundation Stone

CONCLUDING RITE
    General Intercessions
    Lord's Prayer
    Concluding Prayer
    Blessing and Dismissal

RITE OF BLESSING

PART I

APPROACH TO THE CONSTRUCTION SITE

9. The assembly of the people and the approach to the construction site take place, according to circumstances of time and place, in one of the two ways described below.

A. First Form: Procession

10. At a convenient hour the people assemble in a suitable place, from which they will go in procession to the site.

11. The bishop, in his vestments and with the miter and pastoral staff, proceeds with the ministers to the place where the people are assembled. Putting aside the pastoral staff and miter he greets the people, saying:

**The grace of our Lord Jesus Christ
and the love of God
and the fellowship of the Holy Spirit
be with you all.**

R̃. And also with you.

Other suitable words taken preferably from sacred Scripture may be used.

12. Then the bishop briefly instructs the people on their participation in the celebration and explains to them the meaning of the rite.

13. When the bishop has finished the instruction, he says:

Let us pray.

All pray in silence for a brief period. The bishop then continues:

Lord,
you built a holy Church,
founded upon the apostles
with Jesus Christ its cornerstone.

Grant that your people,
gathered in your name,
may fear and love you
and grow as the temple of your glory.

May they always follow you,
until, with you at their head,
they arrive at last in your heavenly city.

We ask this through Christ our Lord.

R. Amen.

14. When the bishop has finished the prayer, he receives the miter and pastoral staff, and, should the occasion demand, the deacon says:

Let us go forth in peace.

The procession takes place in the usual way: the crossbearer leads between two servers with lighted torches; the clergy follow, then the bishop with the assisting deacons and other ministers, and lastly, the congregation. As the procession proceeds the following antiphon is sung with Psalm 84.

My soul is yearning for the courts of the Lord (alleluia).

Another appropriate song may be sung.

Then the reading of the word of God takes place as described below in nos. 18-22.

B. Second Form: Station at the Construction Site of the New Church

15. If the procession cannot take place or seems inappropriate, the people assemble at the construction site of the new church. When the people are assembled the following acclamation is sung.

Eternal peace be yours.
Let the Father's peace unite you in his love.

Abiding peace be yours.
Let the Word be peace to those who bear his name.

Lasting peace be yours.
Let the Spirit's peace comfort all the world.

Another appropriate song may be sung.

■ Meanwhile, the bishop, in his vestments and with miter and pastoral staff, approaches the people. Putting aside the pastoral staff and miter, he greets the people, saying:

The grace of our Lord Jesus Christ
and the love of God
and the fellowship of the Holy Spirit
be with you all.

R. And also with you.

Other suitable words taken preferably from sacred Scripture may be used.

■ **16.** Then the bishop briefly instructs the people on their participation in the celebration and explains to them the meaning of the rite.

■ **17.** When the bishop has finished the instruction, he says:

Let us pray.

All pray in silence for a brief period. The bishop then continues:

Lord,
you built a holy Church,
founded upon the apostles
with Jesus Christ its cornerstone.

Grant that your people,
gathered in your name,
may fear and love you
and grow as the temple of your glory.

May they always follow you,
until, with you at their head,
they arrive at last in your heavenly city.

We ask this through Christ our Lord.

R. Amen.

PART II

READING OF THE WORD OF GOD

18. Then one or more relevant passages of sacred Scripture are read, chosen especially from those in *The Lectionary* (nos. 704 and 706) for the rite of the dedication of a church, with an appropriate intervening responsorial psalm or another appropriate song. However, it is in keeping with the occasion, especially if a foundation stone is used in the rite, to read one of the following passages.

Readings from Sacred Scripture

19.
  1. 1 Kings 5:2-18 "At the king's orders they quarried huge stones, special stones, for the laying of the temple foundations."

  2. Isaiah 28:16-17 "See how I lay in Zion a stone of witness, a precious cornerstone, a foundation stone."

  3. Acts 4:8-12 "Jesus, the one you crucified, has proved to be the keystone."

  4. 1 Corinthians 10:1-6 "And that rock was Christ."

Responsorial Psalms

20.
  1. Psalm 24:1-2, 3-4ab, 5-6
    ℟. (2 Chronicles 7:16a) I have chosen and sanctified this place.

  2. Psalm 42:3, 5bcd; Psalm 43:3-4
    ℟. (See Psalm 43:3) Lord, may your truth lead me to your holy mountain.

  3. Psalm 87:1-3, 4-6, 6-7
    ℟. (See 1) The city of God is founded on the holy mountains.

  4. Psalm 100:2, 3, 5
    ℟. (See Ezechiel 37:27) I will make my dwelling place among the people.

  5. Psalm 118:1-2, 16ab-17, 22-23
    ℟. (See 1 Corinthians 3:11) There is no other foundation than Christ Jesus.

Gospel

21.
  1. Matthew 7:21-29 "A house built on rock and a house built on sand."

  2. Matthew 16:13-18 "On this rock I will build my Church."

3. Mark 12:1-12 "It was the stone rejected by the builders that became the keystone."

4. Luke 6:46-49 "He laid the foundation on rock."

22. When the readings are finished the homily is given, in which the biblical readings are elucidated and the significance of the rite explained: Christ is the cornerstone of the Church, and the temple that is going to be built by the living Church of the community of believers will be at once the house of God and the house of God's people.

23. After the homily, according to the custom of the place, the document of the blessing of the foundation stone and of the beginning of the building of the church may be read; it is signed by the bishop and by representatives of those who are going to work on the building of the church, and together with the stone, is enclosed in the foundations.

PART III

BLESSING OF THE SITE OF THE NEW CHURCH

24. When the homily is finished, the bishop takes off the miter, rises, and blesses the site of the new church, saying:

Let us pray.

Lord,
you fill the entire world with your presence
that your name may be hallowed through all the earth.

Bless all those
who have worked or contributed
to provide this site (property, land)
on which a church will be built.

Today may they rejoice in a work just begun,
soon may they celebrate the sacraments in your temple,
and in time to come may they praise you for ever in heaven.

We ask this through Christ our Lord.

R̲. Amen.

25. Then the bishop puts on the miter and sprinkles the site of the new church with holy water. To do this he may stand in the middle of the site or go in procession around the foundations with the ministers; in the latter case the following antiphon is sung with Psalm 48.

> The walls of Jerusalem will be made of precious stones, and its towers built with gems (alleluia).

Another appropriate song may be sung.

PART IV

BLESSING AND LAYING OF THE FOUNDATION STONE

26. When the site has been blessed, if a foundation stone is to be laid, it is blessed and placed in position as described below in nos. 27-29; otherwise the conclusion of the rite takes place immediately as indicated in nos. 30-31.

■ **27.** The bishop goes to the place where the foundation stone is to be laid and, taking off the miter, blesses the stone, saying:

Let us pray.

Father,
the prophet Daniel spoke of your Son,
as a stone wondrously hewn from a mountain.

The apostle Paul spoke of him,
as a stone firmly founded.

Bless + this foundation stone
to be laid in Christ's name.

You appointed him
the beginning and end of all things.

May this work begin, continue,
and be brought to fulfillment in him,
for he is Lord for ever and ever.

℞. Amen.

Then the bishop may sprinkle the stone with holy water and incense it. Afterward he receives the miter again.

■ **28.** When he has finished, the bishop lays the stone on the foundations in silence or, if he wishes, saying these or similar words:

With faith in Jesus Christ
we lay this stone
on which a church will rise.

May it be a place of sacrament
and a source of grace
to the glory of the Father
who with the Son and Holy Spirit
lives and reigns for ever and ever.

R. Amen.

29. A stone mason then fixes the stone in with mortar. Meanwhile, if the occasion demands, the following antiphon is sung.

The house of the Lord is firmly built on solid rock (alleluia).

Another appropriate song may be sung.

CONCLUDING RITE

■ **30.** When the singing is finished, the bishop takes off the miter, and invites the people to pray the general intercessions, in these or similar words:

Brothers and sisters, now that we have laid the cornerstone of our new church, let us pray to God, our Father.

All pray in silence for a brief period.

That he may transform into a living temple of his glory all whom he has gathered here and who look upon Christ as the cornerstone of their faith, let us pray to the Lord:
R. Bless and watch over your Church, O Lord.

That God in his power may overcome the division and sin which separate his people so that they may ultimately worship as one, let us pray to the Lord: R.

That he may ground upon the bedrock of his Church the faith of all those who have undertaken to work on this building, let us pray to the Lord: R.

That those who are prevented from building places of worship may bear witness to the Lord by conducting themselves as living temples of glory and faith, let us pray to the Lord: R.

That all here present may be cleansed by his divine power and come to share in the celebration of his holy mysteries, let us pray to the Lord: R.

■ Then the bishop may introduce the Lord's Prayer in these or similar words:

Let us join the voice of the Church with that of Christ in praying to the Father using those words which the Son has given us. And so, with one voice, let us say:

Our Father...

■ The bishop continues immediately:

God of love,
we praise your holy name,
for you have made us your temple by baptism
and inspire us to build on earth
churches dedicated to your worship.

Look favorably upon your children,
for they have come with joy
to begin work on this new church.

Enable them to grow into the temple of your glory,
until, shaped anew by your grace,
they are gathered by your hand into your heavenly city.

We ask this through Christ our Lord.

R. Amen.

■ **31.** When the bishop has received the miter and pastoral staff, he blesses the people in the usual way.

The deacon dismisses them, saying:

Go in peace.

R. Thanks be to God.

CHAPTER TWO

DEDICATION OF A CHURCH

INTRODUCTION

I. NATURE AND DIGNITY OF CHURCHES

1. Through his death and resurrection, Christ became the true and perfect temple[1] of the New Covenant and gathered together a people to be his own.

    This holy people, made one as the Father, Son, and Holy Spirit are one, is the Church,[2] that is, the temple of God built of living stones, where the Father is worshiped in spirit and in truth.[3]

    Rightly, then, from early times "church" has also been the name given to the building in which the Christian community gathers to hear the word of God, to pray together, to receive the sacraments, and to celebrate the eucharist.

2. Because the church is a visible building, it stands as a special sign of the pilgrim Church on earth and reflects the Church dwelling in heaven.

    When a church is erected as a building destined solely and permanently for assembling the people of God and for carrying out sacred functions, it is fitting that it be dedicated to God with a solemn rite, in accordance with the ancient custom of the Church.

3. The very nature of a church demands that it be suited to sacred celebrations, dignified, evincing a noble beauty, not mere costly display, and it should stand as a sign and symbol of heavenly realities. "The general plan of the sacred edifice should be such that in some way it conveys the image of the gathered assembly. It should also allow the participants to take the place most appropriate to them and assist all to carry out their individual functions properly." Moreover, in what concerns the sanctuary, the altar, the chair, the lectern, and the place for the reservation of the blessed sacrament, the norms of the General Instruction of the Roman Missal are to be followed.[4]

    Also, the norms must be observed that concern things and places destined for the celebration of other sacraments, especially baptism and penance.[5]

---

[1] See Jn 2:21.
[2] See Cyprian, *De oratione dominica* 23: PL 4, 553; LG, no. 4: AAS 57 (1965) 7; ConstDecrDel 96.
[3] See Jn 4:23.
[4] See GIRM, nos. 253, 257, 258, 259-267, 271, 272, 276-277. See also Roman Ritual, *Holy Communion and Worship of the Eucharist outside Mass*, nos. 6 and 9-11.
[5] See *Rite of Baptism for Children*, no. 25; *Rite of Penance*, no. 12.

II. Titular of a Church and the Relics
of the Saints to be Placed in It

4. Every church to be dedicated must a have a titular. This may be: the Blessed Trinity; our Lord Jesus Christ invoked according to a mystery of his life or a title already accepted in the liturgy; the Holy Spirit; the Blessed Virgin Mary, likewise invoked according to some appellation already accepted in the liturgy; one of the angels; or, finally, a saint inscribed in the Roman Martyrology or in a duly approved Appendix. A blessed may not be the titular without an indult of the Apostolic See. A church should have one titular only, unless it is a question of saints who are listed together in the Calendar.

5. The tradition in the Roman liturgy of placing relics of martyrs or other saints beneath the altar should be preserved, if possible.[6] But the following should be noted:

a) Such relics should be of a size sufficient for them to be recognized as parts of human bodies. Hence excessively small relics of one or more saints must not be placed beneath the altar.

b) The greatest care must be taken to determine whether the relics in question are authentic. It is better for an altar to be dedicated without relics than to have relics of doubtful authenticity placed beneath it.

c) A reliquary must not be placed upon the altar or set into the table of the altar; it must be placed beneath the table of the altar, as the design of the altar permits.

III. Celebration of the Dedication

Minister of the Rite

6. Since the bishop has been entrusted with the care of the particular Church, it is his responsibility to dedicate to God new churches built in his diocese.

If he cannot himself preside at the rite, he shall entrust this function to another bishop, especially to one who is his associate and assistant in the pastoral care of the community for which the church has been built or, in altogether special circumstances, to a priest, to whom he shall give a special mandate.

Choice of Day

7. A day should be chosen for the dedication of the new church when the people can be present in large numbers, especially a Sunday. Since the theme of the dedication pervades this entire rite, the dedication of a new church may not take place on days on which it is altogether improper to

---

[6] See GIRM, no. 266.

disregard the mystery then being commemorated: the Easter triduum, Christmas, Epiphany, Ascension, Pentecost, Ash Wednesday, the weekdays of Holy Week, and All Souls.

Mass of the Dedication

8.   The celebration of the eucharist is inseparably bound up with the rite of the dedication of a church; when a church is dedicated therefore the liturgical texts of the day are omitted and texts proper to the rite are used for both the liturgy of the word and the liturgy of the eucharist.

9.   It is fitting that the bishop concelebrate the Mass with the priests who take part with him in the rite of dedication and those who have been given charge over the parish or the community for which the church has been built.

Office of the Dedication

10.   the day on which a church is dedicated is kept as a solemnity in that church.

The office of the dedication of a church is celebrated, beginning with Evening Prayer I. When the rite of depositing relics takes place, it is highly recommended to keep a vigil at the relics of the martyr or saint that are to be placed beneath the altar; the best way of doing this is to have the office of readings, taken from the respective common or proper. This vigil should be properly adapted to encourage the people's participation, but the requirements of the law are respected.[7]

Parts of the Rite

A. Entrance into the Church

11.   The rite of the dedication begins with the entrance into the church; this may take place in one of the three following ways; the one best suited to the circumstances of time and place is to be used.

— Procession to the church to be dedicated: all assemble in a nearby church or other suitable place, from which the bishop, the ministers, and the congregation proceed to the church to be dedicated, praying and singing.

— Solemn entrance: if the procession cannot take place or seems inopportune, the community gathers at the entrance of the church.

— Simple entrance: the congregation assembles in the church itself; the bishop, the concelebrants, and the ministers enter from the sacristy in the usual way.

---

[7] See GILH, nos. 70-73.

Two rituals are most significant in the entrance into a new church:

a) the handing over of the church: representatives of those who have been involved in the building of the church hand it over to the bishop.

b) The sprinkling of the church: the bishop blesses water and with it sprinkles the people, who are the spiritual temple, then the walls of the church, and finally, the altar.

B. Liturgy of the Word

12. Three readings are used in the liturgy of the word. The texts are chosen from those in the Lectionary (nos. 704 and 706) for the rite of the dedication of a church.

The first reading is always, even during the Easter season, the passage of Nehemiah that tells of the people of Jerusalem gathered in the presence of the scribe Ezra to hear the proclamation of the law of God (Neh 8:1-4a,5-6,8-10).

13. After the readings the bishop gives the homily, in which he explains the biblical readings and the meaning of the dedication of a church.

The profession of faith is always said. The general intercessions are omitted, since the Litany of the Saints is sung in their place.

C. Prayer of Dedication and the Anointing of the Church and the Altar

Depositing of the Relics of the Saints

14. If it is to take place, the relics of a martyr are deposited after the singing of the Litany of the Saints, to signify that the sacrifice of the members has its source in the sacrifice of the Head.[8] When relics of a martyr are not available, relics of another saint may be deposited in the altar.

Prayer of Dedication

15. The celebration of the eucharist is the most important and the one necessary rite for the dedication of a church.

Nevertheless, in accordance with the tradition of the Church in both East and West, a special prayer of dedication is also said. This prayer is a sign of the intention to dedicate the church to the Lord for all times and a petition for his blessing.

---

[8] See RM, Common of Martyrs 8, prayer over the gifts. Ambose, *Epistula* 22:13: PL 16, 1023: "Let the triumphant victims rest in the place where Christ is victim: he, however, who suffered for all, upon the altar; they, who have been redeemed by his sufferings, beneath the altar." See Ps. Maximus of Turin, *Sermo* 78: PL 57, 689-690. Rv 6:9 "I saw underneath the altar the souls of all people who had been killed on account of the word of God, for witnessing to it."

Rites of Anointing, Incensing, Covering, and Lighting the Altar

16. The rites of anointing, incensing, covering, and lighting the altar express in visible signs several aspects of the invisible work that the Lord accomplishes through the Church in its celebration of the divine mysteries, especially the eucharist.

a) *Anointing* of the altar and the walls of the church:

—The anointing with chrism makes the altar a symbol of Christ, who, before all others, is and is called "The Anointed One"; for the Father anointed him with the Holy Spirit and constituted him the High Priest so that on the altar of his body he might offer the sacrifice of his life for the salvation of all.

—The anointing of the church signifies that it is given over entirely and perpetually to Christian worship. In keeping with liturgical tradition, there are twelve anointings, or, where it is more convenient, four, as a symbol that the church is an image of the holy city of Jerusalem.

b) *Incense* is burned on the altar to signify that Christ's sacrifice, there perpetuated in mystery, ascends to God as an odor of sweetness and also to signify that the people's prayers rise up pleasing and acceptable, reaching the throne of God.[9]

The incensation of the nave of the church indicates that the dedication makes it a house of prayer, but the people of God are incensed first, because they are the living temple in which each fanciful member is a spiritual altar.[10]

c) *The covering of the altar* indicates that the Christian altar is the altar of the eucharistic sacrifice and the table of the Lord; around it priests and people, by one and the same rite but with a difference of function, celebrate the memorial of Christ's death and resurrection and partake of his supper. For this reason the altar is prepared as the table of the sacrificial banquet and adorned as for a feast. Thus the dressing of the altar clearly signifies that it is the Lord's table at which all God's people joyously meet to be refreshed with divine food, namely, the body and blood of Christ sacrificed.

d) *The lighting of the altar,* which is followed by the lighting of the church, reminds us that Christ is "a light to enlighten the nations";[11] his brightness shines out in the Church and through it in the whole human family.

D. Celebration of the Eucharist

17. After the altar had been prepared, the bishop celebrates the eucharist, the principal and the most ancient part of the whole rite,[12] because the celebration of the eucharist is in the closest harmony with the rite of the dedication of a church:

—For the celebration of the eucharistic sacrifice achieves the end for which the church was built and the altar erected and expresses this end by particularly clear signs.

---

[9] See Rv 8:3-4.
[10] See Rom 12:1.
[11] Lk 2:32.
[12] See Pope Vigilius, *Epistula ad Profuturum episcopum* 4: PL 84, 832.

— Furthermore, the eucharist, which sanctifies the hearts of those who receive it, in a sense consecrates the altar and the place of celebration, as the ancient Fathers of the Church often assert: "This altar should be an object of awe: by nature it is stone, but it is made holy when it receives the body of Christ."[13]

— Finally, the bond closely connecting the dedication of a church with the celebration of the eucharist is likewise evident from the fact that the Mass for the dedication has its own preface, which is a central part of the rite itself.

IV. ADAPTATION OF THE RITE

Adaptations within the Competence of the Conferences of Bishops

18. The conferences of bishops may adapt this rite, as required, to the character of each region, but in such a way that nothing of its dignity and solemnity is lost.

However, the following are to be respected:

a) The celebration of Mass with the proper preface and prayer for a dedication must never be omitted.

b) Rites that have a special meaning and force from liturgical tradition (see no. 16) must be retained, unless weighty reasons stand in the way, but the wording may be suitably adapted if necessary.

With regard to adaptations, the competent ecclesiastical authority is to consult the Holy See and introduce adaptations with its consent.[14]

Adaptations within the Competence of the Ministers

19. It is for the bishop and for those in charge of the celebration of the rite:

— to decide the manner of entrance into the church (see no. 11);

— to determine the manner of handing over the new church to the bishop (no. 11);

— to decide whether to have the depositing of relics of the saints. The decisive consideration is the spiritual good of the community; the prescriptions in no. 5 must be followed.

It is for the rector of the church to be dedicated, helped by those who assist him in the pastoral work, to decide and prepare everything concerning the readings, singing, and other pastoral aids to foster the fruitful participation of the people and to ensure a dignified celebration.

---

[13] John Chrysostom, *Homilia 20 in 2 Cor 3*: PG 61, 540.
[14] See SC, art. 40.

V. PASTORAL PREPARATION

20. In order that the people may take part fully in the rite of dedication, the rector of the church to be dedicated and others experienced in the pastoral ministry are to instruct them on the import of the celebration and its spiritual, ecclesial, and evangelizing power.

Accordingly, the people are to be instructed about the various parts of the church and their use, the rite of dedication, and the chief liturgical symbols employed in it. Thus led by suitable pastoral resources to a full understanding of the meaning of the dedication of a church through its rites and prayers, they will take an active, intelligent, and devout part in the sacred service.

VI. REQUISITES FOR THE DEDICATION OF A CHURCH

21. For the celebration of the rite the following should be prepared:

a) *In the place of assembly:*

— The Roman Pontifical;

— processional cross;

— if relics of the saints are to be carried in procession, the items in no. 24a.

b) *In the sacristy or in the sanctuary or in the body of the church to be dedicated*, as each situation requires:

— The Roman Missal;

— The Lectionary;

— container of water to be blessed and sprinkler;

— container with the chrism;

— towels for wiping the table of the altar;

— if needed, a waxed linen cloth or waterproof covering of the same size as the altar;

— basin and jug of water, towels, and all that is needed for washing the bishop's hands and those of the priests after they have anointed the walls of the church;

— linen gremial;

— brazier for burning incense or aromatic spices; or grains of incense and small candles to burn on the altar;

— censer, incense boat and spoon;

— chalice, corporal, purificators, and hand towel;

— bread, wine, and water for the celebration of Mass;

— altar cross, unless there is already a cross in the sanctuary or the cross that is carried in the entrance procession is to be placed

— near the altar;

— altar cloth, candles, and candlesticks;

— flowers, if opportune.

22. It is praiseworthy to keep the ancient custom of hanging on the walls of the church crosses made of stone, brass, or other suitable material or of having the crosses carved on the walls. Thus twelve or four crosses should be provided, depending on the number of anointings (see no. 16), and fixed here and there at a suitable height on the walls of the church. Beneath each cross a small bracket should be fitted and in it a small candlestick is placed, with a candle to be lighted.

23. For the Mass of the dedication the vestments are white or of some festive color. The following should be prepared:

— for the bishop: alb, stole, chasuble, miter, pastoral staff, and pallium, if the bishop has the right to wear one;

— for the concelebrating priests: the vestments for concelebrating Mass;

— for the deacons: albs, stoles, and dalmatics;

— for other ministers: albs or other lawfully approved dress.

24. If relics of the saints are to be placed beneath the altar, the following should be prepared:

a) *In the place of assembly:*

— reliquary containing the relics, placed between flowers and lights. When the simple entrance is used, the reliquary may be placed in a suitable part of the sanctuary before the rite begins;

— for the deacons who will carry the relics to be deposited: albs, red stoles, if the relics are those of a martyr, or white in other cases, and, if available, dalmatics. If the relics are carried by priests, then in place of dalmatics chasubles should be prepared.

The relics may also be carried by other ministers, vested in albs or other lawfully approved dress.

b) *In the sanctuary:*

— a small table on which the reliquary is placed during the first part of the dedication rite.

c) *In the sacristy:*

— a sealant or cement to close the cover of the aperture. In addition, a stonemason should be on hand to close the depository of the relics at the proper time.

25. The record of the dedication of the church should be drawn up in duplicate, signed by the bishop, the rector of the church, and representatives of the local community; one copy is to be kept in the diocesan archives, the other in the archives of the church. Where the depositing of relics takes place, a third copy of the record should be made, to be placed at the proper time in the reliquary.

In this record mention should be made of the day, month, and year of the church's dedication, the name of the bishop who celebrated the rite, also the titular of the church and, where applicable, the names of the martyrs or saints whose relics have been deposited beneath the altar.

Moreover, in a suitable place in the church, an inscription should be placed stating the day, month, and year when the dedication took place, the titular of the church, and the name of the bishop who celebrated the rite.

VII. ANNIVERSARY OF THE DEDICATION

A. Anniversary of the Dedication of the Cathedral Church

26. In order that the importance and dignity of the local Church may stand out with greater clarity, the anniversary of the dedication of its cathedral is to be celebrated, with the rank of a solemnity in the cathedral itself, with the rank of a feast in the other churches of the diocese, on the date on which the dedication of the church recurs.[15] If this date is always impeded, the celebration is assigned to the nearest date open. It is desirable that in the cathedral church on the anniversary the bishop concelebrate the eucharist with the chapter of canons or the priests' senate and with the participation of as many of the people as possible.

B. Anniversary of the Dedication of a Particular Church

27. The anniversary of a church's dedication is celebrated with the rank of a solemnity.[16]

---

[15] See GNLYC, Table of Liturgical Days, I, 4b and II, 8b.
[16] See GNLYC, Table of Liturgical Days, I, 4b.

OUTLINE OF THE RITE

INTRODUCTORY RITES

A. First Form: Procession
    Greeting
    Brief Address
    Procession
    Handing Over the Building
    Entrance into the Church

B. Second Form: Solemn Entrance
    Greeting
    Brief Address
    Handing Over the Building
    Entrance into the Church

C. Third Form: Simple Entrance
    Entrance Procession
    Greeting
    Handing Over the Building

    Blessing and Sprinkling of Water
    Hymn: Gloria
    Opening Prayer

LITURGY OF THE WORD
    Presentation of the Lectionary
    First Reading
    Responsorial Psalm
    Second Reading
    Gospel Acclamation
    Gospel
    Homily
    Profession of Faith

PRAYER OF DEDICATION AND THE ANOINTINGS
    Invitation to Prayer
    Litany of the Saints
    Concluding Prayer
    [Depositing of the Relics]
    Prayer of Dedication
    Anointing of the Altar and the Walls of the Church
    Incensation of the Altar and the Church
    Lighting of the Altar and the Church

LITURGY OF THE EUCHARIST
    Preparation of the Altar and the Gifts
    Prayer over the Gifts
    Eucharistic Prayer

    Communion
    [Inauguration of the Blessed Sacrament Chapel
        Prayer after Communion
        Procession to the Chapel
        Incensation of the Eucharist]
    Prayer after Communion

CONCLUDING RITE
    Blessing and Dismissal

RITE OF DEDICATION

PART I

INTRODUCTORY RITES

Entrance into the Church

28. The entry into the church to be dedicated is made, according to circumstances of time and place, in one of the three ways described below.

A. First Form: Procession

29. The door of the church to be dedicated should be closed. At a convenient hour the people assemble in a neighboring church or other suitable place from which the procession may proceed to the church. The relics of the martyrs or saints, if they are to be placed beneath the altar, are prepared in the place where the people assemble.

30. The bishop, the concelebrating priests, the deacons, and ministers, each in appropriate vestments, proceed to the place where the people are assembled. Putting aside the pastoral staff and miter, the bishop greets the people, saying:

**The grace and peace of God
be with all of you
in his holy Church.**

℞. **And also with you.**

Other suitable words taken preferably from sacred Scripture may be used.

Then the bishop addresses the people in these or similar words:

Brothers and sisters in Christ, this is a day of rejoicing: we have come together to dedicate this church by offering within it the sacrifice of Christ.

▶

May we open our hearts and minds to receive his word with faith; may our fellowship born in the one font of baptism and sustained at the one table of the Lord, become the one temple of his Spirit, as we gather round his altar in love.

31. When he has finished addressing the people, the bishop receives the miter and pastoral staff and the procession to the church to be dedicated begins. No lights are used apart from those which surround the relics of the saints, nor is incense used either in the procession or in the Mass before the rite of the incensation and the lighting of the altar and the church (see below, nos. 66-71). The crossbearer leads the procession; the ministers follow; then the deacons or priests with the relics of the saints, ministers, or the faithful accompanying them on either side with lighted torches; then the concelebrating priests; then the bishop with two deacons; and lastly, the congregation.

32. As the procession proceeds, the following antiphon is sung with Psalm 122.

Let us go rejoicing to the house of the Lord.

Another appropriate song may be sung.

33. At the threshold of the church the procession comes to a halt. Representatives of those who have been involved in the building of the church (members of the parish or of the diocese, contributors, architects, workers) hand over the building to the bishop, offering him according to place and circumstances either the legal documents for possession of the building, or the keys, or the plan of the building, or the book in which the progress of the work is described and the names of those in charge of it and the names of the workers recorded. One of the representatives addresses the bishop and the community in a few words, pointing out, if need be, what the new church expresses in its art and in its own special design.

■　　If the door is closed, the bishop then calls upon the priest to whom the pastoral care of the church has been entrusted to open the door.

■　**34.** When the door is unlocked, the bishop invites the people to enter the church in these or similar words:

Go within his gates giving thanks, enter his courts with songs of praise.

Then, preceded by the crossbearer, the bishop and the assembly enter the church. As the procession enters, the following antiphon is sung with Psalm 24.

Lift high the ancient portals. The King of glory enters.

Another appropriate song may be sung.

35. The bishop, without kissing the altar, goes to the chair; the concelebrants, deacons, and ministers go to the places assigned to them in the sanctuary. The relics of the saints are placed in a suitable part of the sanctuary between lighted torches. Water is then blessed with the rite described below, nos. 48-50.

B. Second Form: Solemn Entrance

36. If the procession cannot take place or seems inappropriate, the people assemble at the door of the church to be dedicated, where the relics of the saints have been placed beforehand.

37. Preceded by the crossbearer, the bishop and the concelebrating priests, the deacons, and the ministers, each in appropriate vestments, approach the church door, where the people are assembled. The door of the church should be closed, and the bishop, concelebrants, deacons, and ministers should approach it from outside.

38. Putting aside the pastoral staff and miter, the bishop greets the people, saying:

The grace and peace of God
be with all of you
in his holy Church.

R. And also with you.

Other suitable words taken preferably from sacred Scripture may be used.

Then the bishop addresses the people in these or similar words:

Brothers and sisters in Christ, this is a day of rejoicing: we have come together to dedicate this church by offering within it the sacrifice of Christ.

May we open our hearts and minds to receive his word with faith; may our fellowship born in the one font of baptism and sustained at the one table of the Lord, become the one temple of his Spirit, as we gather round his altar in love.

39. When the bishop has finished addressing the people, he puts on the miter, and, if it seems appropriate, the following antiphon is sung with Psalm 122.

Let us go rejoicing to the house of the Lord.

Another appropriate song may be sung.

40. Then representatives of those who have been involved in the building of the church (members of the parish or of the diocese, contributors, architects, workers) hand over the building to the bishop, offering him according to place and circumstances either the legal documents for possession of the building, or the keys, or the plan of the building, or the book in which the progress of the work is described and the names of those in charge of it and the names of the workers recorded. One of the representatives addresses the bishop and the community in a few words, pointing out, if need be, what the new church expresses in its art and in its own special design.

■ If the door is closed, the bishop then calls upon the priest to whom the pastoral care of the church has been entrusted to open the door.

■ **41.** The bishop takes the pastoral staff and invites the people to enter the church in these or similar words:

Go within his gates giving thanks, enter his courts with songs of praise.

Then, preceded by the crossbearer, the bishop and the assembly enter the church. As the procession enters, the following antiphon is sung with Psalm 24.

Lift high the ancient portals. The King of glory enters.

Another appropriate song may be sung.

■ **42.** The bishop, without kissing the altar, goes to the chair; the concelebrants, deacons, and ministers go to the places assigned to them in the sanctuary. The relics of the saints are placed in a suitable part of the sanctuary between lighted torches. Water is then blessed with the rite described below, in nos. 48-50.

C. Third Form: Simple Entrance

43. If the solemn entrance cannot take place, the simple entrance is used. When the people are assembled, the bishop and the concelebrating priests, the deacons, and the ministers, each in appropriate vestments, preceded by the crossbearer, go from the sacristy through the main body of the church to the sanctuary.

44. If there are relics of the saints to be placed beneath the altar, these are brought in the entrance procession to the sanctuary from the sacristy or the chapel where since the vigil they have been exposed for the veneration of the people. For a just cause, before the celebration begins, the relics may be placed between lighted torches in a suitable part of the sanctuary.

45. As the procession proceeds, the entrance antiphon is sung with Psalm 122.

God in his holy dwelling, God who has gathered us together in his house: he will strengthen and console his people.

Or:

Let us go rejoicing to the house of the Lord.

Another appropriate song may be sung.

■ **46.** When the procession reaches the sanctuary, the relics of the saints are placed between lighted torches in a suitable place. The concelebrating priests, the deacons, and the ministers go to the places assigned to them; the bishop, without kissing the altar, goes to the chair. Then, putting aside the pastoral staff and miter, he greets the people, saying:

**The grace and peace of God
be with all of you
in his holy Church.**

R. And also with you.

Other suitable words taken preferably from sacred Scripture may be used.

47. Then representatives of those who have been involved in the building of the church (members of the parish or of the diocese, contributors, architects, workers) hand over the building to the bishop, offering him according to place and circumstances either the legal documents for possession of the building, or the keys, or the plan of the building, or the book in which the progress of the work is described and the names of those in charge of it and the names of the workers recorded. One of the representatives addresses the bishop and the community in a few words, pointing out, if need be, what the new church expresses in its art and in its own special design.

Blessing and Sprinkling of Water

■ **48.** When the entrance rite is completed, the bishop blesses water with which to sprinkle the people as a sign of repentance and as a reminder of their baptism, and to purify the walls and the altar of the new church. The ministers bring the vessel with the water to the bishop who stands at the chair. The bishop invites all to pray, in these or similar words:

Brothers and sisters in Christ, in this solemn rite of dedication, let us ask the Lord our God to bless this water created by his hand.

It is a sign of our repentance, a reminder of our baptism, and a symbol of the cleansing of these walls and this altar.

May the grace of God help us to remain faithful members of his Church, open to the Spirit we have received.

■ All pray in silence for a brief period. The bishop then continues:

God of mercy,
you call every creature to the light of life,
and surround us with such great love
that when we stray
you continually lead us back to Christ our head.

For you have established an inheritance of such mercy,
that those sinners, who pass through water made sacred,
die with Christ and rise restored
as members of his body
and heirs of his eternal covenant.

Bless + this water;
sanctify it.

As it is sprinkled upon us and throughout this church
make it a sign of the saving waters of baptism,
by which we become one in Christ, the temple of your Spirit.

May all here today,
and all those in days to come,
who will celebrate your mysteries in this church,
be united at last in the holy city of your peace.

We ask this in the name of Jesus the Lord.

℟. Amen.

■ **49.** The bishop, accompanied by the deacons, passes through the main body of the church, sprinkling the people and the walls with the holy water; then, when he has returned to the sanctuary, he sprinkles the altar. Meanwhile the following antiphon is sung.

I saw water flowing from the right side of the temple, alleluia. It brought God's life and his salvation, and the people sang in joyful praise: alleluia, alleluia.

Or, during Lent:

I will pour clean water over you and wash away all your defilement. A new heart will I give you, says the Lord.

Another appropriate song may be sung.

50. After the sprinkling the bishop returns to the chair and, when the singing is finished, standing with hands joined, says:

May God, the Father of mercies,
dwell in this house of prayer.
May the grace of the Holy Spirit cleanse us,
for we are the temple of his presence.

℟. Amen.

Hymn

51. Then the **Gloria** is sung.

Opening Prayer

52. When the hymn is finished, the bishop, with hands joined, says:

Let us pray.

All pray in silence for a brief period. Then the bishop, with hands extended, says:

Lord,
fill this place with your presence,
and extend your hand
to all those who call upon you.

May your word here proclaimed
and your sacraments here celebrated
strengthen the hearts of all the faithful.

We ask this through our Lord Jesus Christ, your Son,
who lives and reigns with you and the Holy Spirit,
one God, for ever and ever.

℟. Amen.

PART II

LITURGY OF THE WORD

■ **53.** The proclamation of the word of God is fittingly carried out in this way: two readers, one of whom carries *The Lectionary*, and the psalmist come to the bishop. The bishop, standing with the miter on, takes *The Lectionary*, shows it to the people, and says:

**May the word of God always be heard in this place,
as it unfolds the mystery of Christ before you
and achieves your salvation within the Church.**

R. Amen.

■ Then the bishop hands *The Lectionary* to the first reader. The readers and the psalmist proceed to the lectern, carrying *The Lectionary* for all to see.

54. The readings are arranged in this way:

a) The first reading is always taken from the Book of Nehemiah 8:1-4a, 5-6, 8-10, followed by the singing of Psalm 19B:8-9, 10, 15 with the response:

R. Your words, Lord, are spirit and life.

b) The second reading and the gospel are taken from the texts in *The Lectionary* (nos. 701-706) for the rite of the dedication of a church. Neither lights nor incense are carried at the gospel.

55. After the gospel the bishop gives the homily, in which he explains the biblical readings and the meaning of the rite.

56. The profession of faith is said. The general intercessions are omitted since in their place the litany of the saints is sung.

PART III

PRAYER OF DEDICATION AND THE ANOINTINGS

Invitation to Prayer

■ **57.** Then all stand, and the bishop, without his miter, invites the people to pray in these or similar words:

Let us ask the saints to support our prayers to God the Father almighty, who has made the hearts of his people faithful temples of his Spirit.

Deacon (except on Sundays and during the Easter season):

Let us kneel.

Litany of the Saints

58. Then the litany of the saints is sung, with all responding. On Sundays and also during the Easter season, all stand; on other days, all kneel.

59. The cantors begin the litany (appendix, p. 104); they add, at the proper place, names of other saints (the titular of the church, the patron saint of the place, and the saints whose relics are to be deposited, if this is to take place) and petitions suitable to the occasion.

■ **60.** When the litany is finished, the bishop, standing with hands extended, says:

Lord,
may the prayers of the Blessed Virgin Mary
and of all the saints
make our prayers acceptable to you.

May this building,
which we dedicate to your name,
be a house of salvation and grace
where Christians gathered in fellowship
may worship you in spirit and truth
and grow together in love.

Grant this through Christ our Lord.

R. Amen.

If it is applicable, the deacon says:

Let us stand.

All rise. The bishop receives the miter.

When there is no depositing of the relics of the saints, the bishop immediately says the prayer of dedication as indicated in no. 62 below.

Depositing of the Relics

■ **61.** Then, if relics of the martyrs or other saints are to be placed beneath the altar, the bishop approaches the altar. A deacon or priest brings them to the bishop, who places them in a suitably prepared aperture. Meanwhile one of the following antiphons is sung with Psalm 15.

> Saints of God, you have been enthroned at the foot of God's altar; pray for us to the Lord Jesus Christ.

> Or:

> The bodies of the saints lie buried in peace, but their names will live on for ever (alleluia).

> Another appropriate song may be sung.

> Meanwhile a stone mason closes the aperture and the bishop returns to the chair.

Prayer of Dedication

■ **62.** Then the bishop, standing without miter at the chair or near the altar, with hands extended, says:

Father in heaven,
source of holiness and true purpose,
it is right that we praise and glorify your name.

For today we come before you,
to dedicate to your lasting service
this house of prayer, this temple of worship,
this home in which we are nourished by your word
   and your sacraments.

Here is reflected the mystery of the Church.

The Church is fruitful,
made holy by the blood of Christ:
a bride made radiant with his glory,
a virgin splendid in the wholeness of her faith,
a mother blessed through the power of the Spirit.

The Church is holy,
your chosen vineyard:
its branches envelop the world,
its tendrils, carried on the tree of the cross,
reach up to the kingdom of heaven.

34

The Church is favored,
the dwelling place of God on earth:
a temple built of living stones,
founded on the apostles
with Jesus Christ its corner stone.

The Church is exalted,
a city set on a mountain:
a beacon to the whole world,
bright with the glory of the Lamb,
and echoing the prayers of her saints.

Lord,
send your Spirit from heaven
to make this church an ever-holy place,
and this altar a ready table for the sacrifice of Christ.

Here may the waters of baptism
overwhelm the shame of sin;
here may your people die to sin
and live again through grace as your children.

Here may your children,
gathered around your altar,
celebrate the memorial of the Paschal Lamb,
and be fed at the table
of Christ's word and Christ's body.

Here may prayer, the Church's banquet,
resound through heaven and earth
as a plea for the world's salvation.

Here may the poor find justice,
the victims of oppression, true freedom.

From here may the whole world
clothed in the dignity of the children of God,
enter with gladness your city of peace.

We ask this through our Lord Jesus Christ, your Son,
who lives and reigns with you and the Holy Spirit,
one God, for ever and ever.

℟. Amen.

Anointing of the Altar and the Walls of the Church

■ **63.** Then the bishop, removing the chasuble if necessary and putting on a linen gremial, goes to the altar with the deacons and other ministers, one of whom carries the chrism. The bishop proceeds to anoint the altar and the walls of the church as described in no. 64 below.

If the bishop wishes to associate some of the concelebrating priests with him in the anointing of the walls, after the anointing of the altar, he hands them vessels of sacred chrism and goes with them to complete the anointings.

However, the bishop may give the task of anointing the walls to the priests alone; in that case, he hands the vessels of sacred chrism to them after he has anointed the altar.

■ **64.** The bishop, standing before the altar, says:

We now anoint this altar and this building.
May God in his power make them holy,
visible signs of the mystery of Christ and his Church.

Then he pours chrism on the middle of the altar and on each of its four corners, and it is recommended that he anoint the entire table of the altar with this.

When the altar has been anointed, the bishop anoints the walls of the church, signing with chrism the suitably distributed twelve or four crosses. He may have the assistance of two or four priests.

If the anointing of the walls is given to the priests, after the bishop has anointed the altar, they anoint the walls of the church signing the crosses with chrism.

Meanwhile one of the following antiphons is sung with Psalm 84.

See the place where God lives among his people; there the Spirit of God will make his home among you; the temple of God is holy and you are that temple (alleuia).

Or:

Holy is the temple of the Lord, it is God's handiwork, his dwelling place.

Another appropriate song may be sung.

■ **65.** When the altar and walls have been anointed, the bishop returns to the chair, sits, and washes his hands. Then the bishop takes off the gremial and puts on the chasuble. The priests also wash their hands after they have anointed the walls.

Incensation of the Altar and the Church

■ **66.** After the rite of anointing, a brazier is placed on the altar for burning incense or aromatic gums, or, if desired, a heap of incense mixed with small candles or wax tapers is made on the altar. The bishop puts incense into the brazier or he lights the heap of incense with a small candle handed to him by a minister, saying:

Lord,
may our prayer ascend as incense in your sight.
As this building is filled with fragrance
so may your Church fill the world
with the fragrance of Christ.

67. Then the bishop puts incense into some censers and incenses the altar; he returns to the chair, is incensed, and then sits. Ministers, walking through the church, incense the people and the walls.

68. Meanwhile one of the following antiphons is sung with Psalm 138.

An angel stood by the altar of the temple, holding a golden censer.

Or:

From the hand of the angel, clouds of incense rose in the presence of the Lord.

Another appropriate song may be sung.

Lighting of the Altar and the Church

69. After the incensation, a few ministers wipe the table of the altar with cloths, and, if need be, cover it with a waterproof linen. They then cover the altar with a cloth, and, if opportune, decorate it with flowers. They arrange in a suitable manner the candles needed for the celebration of Mass, and, if need be, the cross.

70. Then the bishop gives to the deacon a lighted candle, and says:

Light of Christ,
shine forth in the Church
and bring all nations
to the fullness of truth.

Then the bishop sits. The deacon goes to the altar and lights the candles for the celebration of the eucharist.

71. Then the festive lighting takes place: all the candles, including those at the places where the anointings were made, and the other lamps are lit as a sign of rejoicing. Meanwhile the following antiphon is sung with the canticle of Tobias.

Your light will come, Jerusalem; upon you the glory of the Lord will dawn and all nations will walk in your light, alleluia.

Or, during Lent:

Jerusalem, city of God, you will shine with the light of God's splendor; all people on earth will pay you homage.

Canticle of Tobias

(Vg. 13:10; 13-14ab; 14c-15; 17)

Bless the Lord, all you saints of the Lord.
Rejoice and give him thanks.

(Repeat antiphon)

Jerusalem, city of God,
you will shine with the light of God's splendor;
all people on earth will pay you homage.
Nations will come from afar,
bearing gifts for the King of heaven;
in you they will worship the Lord.

(Repeat antiphon)

Nations will consider your land holy,
for in you they will call upon the great name of the Lord.
You will exult and rejoice over the children of the righteous,
for they will be gathered together to praise the Lord.

(Repeat antiphon)

Another appropriate song may be sung, especially one in honor of Christ, the light of the world.

PART IV

LITURGY OF THE EUCHARIST

72. The deacons and the ministers prepare the altar in the usual way. Then some of the congregation bring bread, wine, and water for the celebration of the Lord's sacrifice. The bishop receives the gifts at the chair. While the gifts are being brought, the following antiphon may be sung:

Lord God, in the simplicity of my heart I have joyously offered all things to you; with great joy I have looked upon your chosen people, Lord God, I have obeyed your will (alleluia).

Another appropriate song may be sung.

■ **73.** When all is ready, the bishop goes to the altar, removes the miter, and kisses the altar. The Mass proceeds in the usual way; however, neither the gifts nor the altar are incensed.

Prayer Over the Gifts

■ **74.** With hands extended, the bishop sings or says:

Lord,
accept the gifts of a rejoicing Church.

May your people,
who are gathered in this sacred place,
arrive at eternal salvation
through the mysteries in which they share.

Grant this through Christ our Lord.

℟. Amen.

Eucharistic Prayer

■ **75.** Eucharistic Prayer I or III is said, with the following preface, which is an integral part of the rite of the dedication of a church. With hands extended the bishop sings or says:

The Lord be with you.

℟. And also with you.

Lift up your hearts.

℟. We lift them up to the Lord.

Let us give thanks to the Lord our God.

℟. It is right to give him thanks and praise.

Father, all-powerful and ever-living God,
we do well always and everywhere to give you thanks.

▶

The whole world is your temple,
shaped to resound with your name.
Yet you also allow us to dedicate to your service
places designed for your worship.

With hearts full of joy
we consecrate to your glory
this work of our hands, this house of prayer.

Here is foreshadowed the mystery of your true temple;
this church is the image on earth of your heavenly city:

For you made the body of your Son
born of the Virgin,
a temple consecrated to your glory,
the dwelling place of your godhead in all its fullness.

You have established the Church as your holy city,
founded on the apostles,
with Jesus Christ its cornerstone.

You continue to build your Church with chosen stones,
enlivened by the Spirit,
and cemented together by love.

In that holy city you will be all in all for endless ages,
and Christ will be its light for ever.

Through Christ we praise you, Lord,
with all the angels and saints in their song of joy:

Holy, holy, holy Lord, God of power and might,
heaven and earth are full of your glory.
    Hosanna in the highest.
Blessed is he who comes in the name of the Lord.
    Hosanna in the highest.

■ **76.** In Eucharistic Prayer I the special form of **Father, accept this offering** is said:

Father,
accept this offering
from your whole family,
and from your servants

who with heart and hand
have given and built this church
as an offering to you (in honor of N.).
Grant us your peace in this life,
save us from final damnation,
and count us among those you have chosen.

77. In the intercessions of Eucharistic Prayer III, after the words, **with . . . the entire people your Son has gained for you,** the following is said:

Father,
accept the prayers of those who dedicate this church to you.

May it be a place of salvation and sacrament
where your Gospel of peace is proclaimed
and your holy mysteries celebrated.

Guided by your word and secure in your peace
may your chosen people now journeying through life
arrive safely at their eternal home.

There may all your children
now scattered abroad
be settled at last in your city of peace.

78. While the bishop is receiving the body of Christ the communion song begins. One of the following antiphons is sung with Psalm 128.

My house shall be called a house of prayer, says the Lord: in it all who ask shall receive, all who seek shall find, and all who knock shall have the door opened to them (alleluia).

Or:

May the children of the Church be like olive branches around the table of the Lord (alleluia).

Another appropriate song may be sung.

If there is no inauguration of the blessed sacrament chapel, the Mass proceeds as below, no. 83.

Inauguration of the Blessed Sacrament Chapel

79. The inauguration of a chapel where the blessed sacrament is to be reserved, is carried out appropriately in this way: after the communion the pyx containing the blessed sacrament is left on the table of the altar. The bishop goes to the chair, and all pray in silence for a brief period. Then the bishop says the following prayer after communion:

Let us pray.

Pause for silent prayer, if this has not preceded.

Lord,
through these gifts
increase the vision of your truth in our minds.

May we always worship you in your holy temple,
and rejoice in your presence with all your saints.

Grant this through Christ our Lord.

R. Amen.

80. When the prayer is completed, the bishop returns to the altar, genuflects, and incenses the blessed sacrament. Afterward, when he has received the humeral veil, he takes the pyx, which he covers with the veil itself. Then a procession is formed in which, preceded by the crossbearer and with lighted torches and incense, the blessed sacrament is carried through the main body of the church to the chapel of reservation. As the procession proceeds, the following antiphon is sung with Psalm 147:12-20.

> **Praise the Lord, Jerusalem.**

Another appropriate song may be sung.

81. When the procession comes to the chapel of reservation, the bishop places the pyx on the altar or in the tabernacle, the door of which remains open. Then he puts incense in the censer, kneels, and incenses the blessed sacrament. Finally, after a brief period during which all pray in silence, the deacon puts the pyx in the tabernacle or closes the door. A minister lights the lamp, which will burn perpetually before the blessed sacrament.

82. If the chapel where the blessed sacrament is reserved can be seen clearly by the congregation, the bishop immediately imparts the blessing of the Mass (see below, no. 84). Otherwise the procession returns to the sanctuary by the shorter route and the bishop imparts the blessing either at the altar or at the chair.

Prayer after Communion

83. If there is no inauguration of the blessed sacrament chapel, when the communion of the congregation is finished, the bishop says:

Let us pray.

Pause for silent prayer, if this has not preceded.

Lord,
through these gifts
increase the vision of your truth in our minds.

May we always worship you in your holy temple,
and rejoice in your presence with all your saints.

Grant this through Christ our Lord.

℟. Amen.

Blessing and Dismissal

■ **84.** The bishop receives the miter and says:

The Lord be with you.

℟. And also with you.

Then the deacon, if appropriate, gives the invitation to the people in these or similar words:

Bow your heads and pray for God's blessing.

■ Then the bishop extends his hands over the people and blesses them, saying:

The Lord of earth and heaven
has assembled you before him this day
to dedicate this house of prayer.
May he fill you with the blessings of heaven.

℟. Amen.

God the Father wills that all his children
scattered through the world
become one family in his Son.
May he make you his temple,
the dwelling place of his Holy Spirit.

℟. Amen. ▶

May God free you from every bond of sin,
dwell within you and give you joy.
May you live with him for ever
in the company of all his saints.

R̷. Amen.

The bishop takes the pastoral staff and continues:

May almighty God bless you,
the Father, and the Son, + and the Holy Spirit.

R̷. Amen.

85. Finally the deacon dismisses the people in the usual way.

CHAPTER THREE

DEDICATION OF A CHURCH IN WHICH MASS IS ALREADY BEING CELEBRATED REGULARLY

INTRODUCTION

1. In order to bring out fully the symbolism and the significance of the rite, the opening of a new church and its dedication should take place at one and the same time. For this reason, as was said before, care should be taken that, as far as possible, Mass is not celebrated in a new church before it is dedicated (see chapter two, nos. 8, 15, 17).

Nevertheless in the case of the dedication of a church where the sacred mysteries are already being celebrated regularly, the rite set out in this chapter must be used.

Moreover, a clear distinction exists in regard to these churches. In the case of those just built the reason for a dedication is obvious. In the case of those standing for some time the following requirements must be met for them to be dedicated:

— that the altar has not already been dedicated, since it is rightly forbidden both by custom and by liturgical law to dedicate a church without dedicating the altar, for the dedication of the altar is the principal part of the whole rite;

— that there be something new or notably altered about the edifice, relative either to its structure (for example, a total restoration) or its status in law (for example, the church's being ranked as a parish church).

2. All the directions given in the Introduction to chapter two apply to this rite, unless they are clearly extraneous to the situation which this rite envisages or other directions are given.

This rite differs chiefly from that described in chapter two on these points:

a) The rite of opening the doors of the church (see chapter two, no. 34 or no. 41) is omitted, since the church is already open to the community; consequently, the entrance rite takes the form of the simple entrance (see chapter two, nos. 43-47). However, in the case of dedicating a church closed for a long time and now being opened again for sacred celebrations, the rite of opening the doors may be carried out, since in this case it retains its point and significance.

b) The rite of handing over the church to the bishop (see chapter two, no. 33 or no. 40 or no. 47), depending on the situation, is either to be followed, omitted, or adapted in a way relevant to the condition of the church being dedicated (for example, it will be right to retain it in dedicating a church built recently; to omit it in dedicating an older church where nothing has been changed in the structure; to adapt it in dedicating an older church completely restored).

c) The rite of sprinkling the church walls with holy water (see chapter two, nos. 48-50), purificatory by its very nature, is omitted.

d) All the rites belonging to the first proclamation of the word of God in a church (see chapter two, no. 53) are omitted; thus the liturgy of the word takes place in the usual way. A different, pertinent reading is chosen in place of Neh 8:1-4a and its responsorial psalm, Ps 19b:8-9,10,15 (see chapter two, no. 54a).

OUTLINE OF THE RITE

INTRODUCTORY RITES
Entrance into the Church
  Entrance Procession
  Greeting
  Handing Over the Building
Blessing and Sprinkling of Water
Hymn: Gloria
Opening Prayer

LITURGY OF THE WORD
First Reading
Responsorial Psalm
Second Reading
Gospel Acclamation
Gospel
Homily
Profession of Faith

PRAYER OF DEDICATION AND THE ANOINTINGS
Invitation to Prayer
Litany of the Saints
Concluding Prayer
[Depositing of the Relics]
Prayer of Dedication
Anointing of the Altar and the Walls of the Church
Incensation of the Altar and the Church
Lighting of the Altar and the Church

LITURGY OF THE EUCHARIST
Preparation of the Altar and the Gifts
Prayer over the Gifts
Eucharistic Prayer

———————

Communion
[Inauguration of the Blessed Sacrament Chapel
  Prayer after Communion
  Procession to the Chapel
  Incensation of the Eucharist]
Prayer after Communion

CONCLUDING RITE
Blessing and Dismissal

RITE OF DEDICATION

PART I

INTRODUCTORY RITES

Entrance into the Church

3. When the people are assembled, the bishop and the concelebrating priests, the deacons, and the ministers, each in appropriate vestments, preceded by the crossbearer, go from the sacristy through the main body of the church to the sanctuary.

4. If there are relics of the saints to be placed beneath the altar, these are brought in the entrance procession to the sanctuary from the sacristy or the chapel where since the vigil they have been exposed for the veneration of the people. For a just cause, before the celebration begins, the relics may be placed between lighted torches in a suitable part of the sanctuary.

5. As the procession proceeds, the entrance antiphon is sung with Psalm 122.

God in his holy dwelling, God who has gathered us together in his house: he will strengthen and console his people.

Or:

Let us go rejoicing to the house of the Lord.

Another appropriate song may be sung.

6. When the procession reaches the sanctuary, the relics of the saints are placed between lighted torches in a suitable place. The concelebrating priests, the deacons, and the ministers go to the places assigned to them; the bishop, without kissing the altar, goes to the chair. Then, putting aside the pastoral staff and miter, he greets the people, saying:

**The grace and peace of God
be with all of you
in his holy Church.**

R. And also with you.

Other suitable words taken preferably from sacred Scripture may be used.

7. If circumstances dictate that the church is to be handed over to the bishop (see Introduction, no.2b), representatives of those who have been involved in the building of the church (members of the parish or of the diocese, contributors, architects, workers) hand over the building to the bishop, offering him either the legal documents for possession of the building, or the keys, or the plan of the building, or the book in which the progress of the work is described and the names of those in charge of it and the names of the workers recorded. One of the representatives addresses the bishop and the community in a few words, pointing out, if need be, what the church expresses in its art and in its own special design.

Blessing and Sprinkling of Water

■ **8.** When the entrance rite is completed, the bishop blesses water with which to sprinkle the people as a sign of repentance and as a reminder of their baptism. The ministers return the vessel with the water to the bishop who stands at the chair. The bishop invites all to pray, in these or similar words:

Brothers and sisters in Christ in this solemn rite of dedication let us ask the Lord our God to bless this water, created by his hand.

It is a sign of our repentance and a reminder of our baptism.

May the grace of God help us to remain faithful members of his Church, open to the Spirit we have received.

■ All pray in silence for a brief period. The bishop then continues:

God of mercy,
you call every creature to the light of life,
and surround us with such great love
that when we stray
you continually lead us back to Christ our head.

For you have established an inheritance of such mercy,
that those sinners, who pass through water made sacred,
die with Christ and rise restored
as members of his body
and heirs of his eternal covenant.

Bless + this water;
sanctify it.

As it is sprinkled upon us and throughout this church
make it a sign of the saving waters of baptism,
by which we become one in Christ, the temple of your Spirit.

May all here today,
and all those in days to come,
who will celebrate your mysteries in this church
be united at last in the holy city of your peace.

We ask this in the name of Jesus the Lord.

℟. Amen.

■ **9.** The bishop, accompanied by the deacons, sprinkles the people with holy water; then if the altar is completely new he sprinkles it too. Meanwhile the following antiphon is sung.

I saw water flowing from the right side of the temple, alleluia. It brought God's life and his salvation, and the people sang in joyful praise: alleluia, alleluia.

Or, during Lent:

I will pour clean water over you and wash away all your defilement. A new heart will I give you, says the Lord.

Another appropriate song may be sung.

■ **10.** After the sprinkling the bishop returns to the chair and, when the singing is finished, standing with hands joined, says:

May God, the Father of mercies,
dwell in this house of prayer.
May the grace of the Holy Spirit cleanse us,
for we are the temple of his presence.

℟. Amen.

Hymn

11. Then the **Gloria** is sung.

Opening Prayer

■ **12.** When the hymn is finished, the bishop, with hands joined, says:

Let us pray.

All pray in silence for a brief period. Then the bishop, with hands extended, says:

Lord,
fill this place with your presence,
and extend your hand
to all those who call upon you.

May your word here proclaimed
and your sacraments here celebrated
strengthen the hearts of all the faithful.

We ask this through our Lord Jesus Christ, your Son,
who lives and reigns with you and the Holy Spirit,
one God, for ever and ever.

R. Amen.

PART II

LITURGY OF THE WORD

13. The bishop sits and receives the miter; the people also are seated. Then the liturgy of the word takes place; the readings are taken from the texts in *The Lectionary* (nos. 701 and 706) for the rite of the dedication of a church.

14. Neither lights nor incense are carried at the gospel.

15. After the gospel the bishop gives the homily, in which he explains the biblical readings and the meaning of the rite.

16. The profession of faith is said. The general intercessions are omitted since in their place the litany of the saints is sung.

PART III

PRAYER OF DEDICATION AND THE ANOINTINGS

Invitation to Prayer

17. Then all stand, and the bishop, without his miter, invites the people to pray in these or similar words:

52

Let us ask the saints to support our prayers to God the Father almighty, who has made the hearts of his people faithful temples of his Spirit.

Deacon (except on Sundays and during the Easter season):

Let us kneel.

Litany of the Saints

18. Then the litany of the saints is sung, with all responding. On Sundays and also during the Easter season, all stand; on other days, all kneel.

19. The cantors begin the litany (appendix, p. 104); they add, at the proper place, names of other saints (the titular of the church, the patron saint of the place, and the saints whose relics are to be deposited, if this is to take place) and petitions suitable to the occasion.

■ **20.** When the litany is finished, the bishop, standing with hands extended, says:

Lord,
may the prayers of the Blessed Virgin Mary
and of all the saints
make our prayers acceptable to you.

May this building,
which we dedicate to your name,
be a house of salvation and grace
where Christians gathered in fellowship
may worship you in spirit and truth
and grow together in love.·
Grant this through Christ our Lord.

℟. Amen.

If it is applicable, the deacon says:

Let us stand.

All rise. The bishop receives the miter.

When there is no depositing of the relics of the saints, the bishop immediately says the prayer of dedication as indicated in no. 22 below.

Depositing of the Relics

■ **21.** Then, if relics of the martyrs or other saints are to be placed beneath the altar, the bishop approaches the altar. A deacon or priest brings them to the bishop, who places them in a suitably prepared aperture. Meanwhile one of the following antiphons is sung with Psalm 15.

> Saints of God, you have been enthroned at the foot of God's altar; pray for us to the Lord Jesus Christ.

> Or:

> The bodies of the saints lie buried in peace, but their names will live on for ever (alleluia).

> Another appropriate song may be sung.

> Meanwhile a stone mason closes the aperture and the bishop returns to the chair.

Prayer of Dedication

■ **22.** Then the bishop, standing without miter at the chair or near the altar, with hands extended, says:

Father in heaven,
source of holiness and true purpose,
it is right that we praise and glorify your name.

For today we come before you,
to dedicate to your lasting service
this house of prayer, this temple of worship,
this home in which we are nourished by your word
    and your sacraments.

Here is reflected the mystery of the Church.

The Church is fruitful,
made holy by the blood of Christ:
a bride made radiant with his glory,
a virgin splendid in the wholeness of her faith,
a mother blessed through the power of the Spirit.

The Church is holy,
your chosen vineyard:
its branches envelop the world,
its tendrils, carried on the tree of the cross,
reach up to the kingdom of heaven.

54

The Church is favored,
the dwelling place of God on earth:
a temple built of living stones,
founded on the apostles
with Jesus Christ its corner stone.

The Church is exalted,
a city set on a mountain:
a beacon to the whole world,
bright with the glory of the Lamb,
and echoing the prayers of her saints.

Lord,
send your Spirit from heaven
to make this church an ever-holy place,
and this altar a ready table for the sacrifice of Christ.

Here may the waters of baptism
overwhelm the shame of sin;
here may your people die to sin
and live again through grace as your children.

Here may your children,
gathered around your altar,
celebrate the memorial of the Paschal Lamb,
and be fed at the table
of Christ's word and Christ's body.

Here may prayer, the Church's banquet,
resound through heaven and earth
as a plea for the world's salvation.

Here may the poor find justice,
the victims of oppression, true freedom.

From here may the whole world
clothed in the dignity of the children of God,
enter with gladness your city of peace.

We ask this through our Lord Jesus Christ, your Son,
who lives and reigns with you and the Holy Spirit,
one God, for ever and ever.

R. Amen.

Anointing of the Altar and the Walls of the Church

■ **23.** Then the bishop, removing the chasuble if necessary and putting on a linen gremial, goes to the altar with the deacons and other ministers, one of whom carries the chrism. The bishop proceeds to anoint the altar and the walls of the church as described in no. 24 below.

If the bishop wishes to associate some of the concelebrating priests with him in the anointing of the walls, after the anointing of the altar, he hands them vessels of sacred chrism and goes with them to complete the anointings.

However, the bishop may give the task of anointing the walls to the priests alone; in that case, he hands the vessels of sacred chrism to them after he has anointed the altar.

24. The bishop, standing before the altar, says:

We now anoint this altar and this building.
May God in his power make them holy,
visible signs of the mystery of Christ and his Church.

Then he pours chrism on the middle of the altar and on each of its four corners, and it is recommended that he anoint the entire table of the altar with this.

When the altar has been anointed, the bishop anoints the walls of the church, signing with chrism the suitably distributed twelve or four crosses. He may have the assistance of two or four priests.

If the anointing of the walls is given to the priests, after the bishop has anointed the altar, they anoint the walls of the church signing the crosses with chrism.

Meanwhile one of the following antiphons is sung with Psalm 84.

See the place where God lives among his people; there the Spirit of God will make his home among you; the temple of God is holy and you are that temple (alleuia).

Or:

Holy is the temple of the Lord, it is God's handiwork, his dwelling place.

Another appropriate song may be sung.

■ **25.** When the altar and walls have been anointed, the bishop returns to the chair, sits, and washes his hands. Then the bishop takes off the gremial and puts on the chasuble. The priests also wash their hands after they have anointed the walls.

Incensation of the Altar and the Church

■ **26.** After the rite of anointing, a brazier is placed on the altar for burning incense or aromatic gums, or, if desired, a heap of incense mixed with small candles or wax tapers is made on the altar. The bishop puts incense into the brazier or he lights the heap of incense with a small candle handed to him by a minister, saying:

Lord,
may our prayer ascend as incense in your sight.
As this building is filled with fragrance
so may your Church fill the world
with the fragrance of Christ.

27. Then the bishop puts incense into some censers and incenses the altar; he returns to the chair, is incensed, and then sits. Ministers, walking through the church, incense the people and the walls.

28. Meanwhile one of the following antiphons is sung with Psalm 138.

An angel stood by the altar of the temple, holding a golden censer.

Or:

From the hand of the angel, clouds of incense rose in the presence of the Lord.

Another appropriate song may be sung.

Lighting of the Altar and the Church

29. After the incensation, a few ministers wipe the table of the altar with cloths, and, if need be, cover it with a waterproof linen. They then cover the altar with a cloth, and, if opportune, decorate it with flowers. They arrange in a suitable manner the candles needed for the celebration of Mass, and, if need be, the cross.

30. Then the bishop gives to the deacon a lighted candle and says:

Light of Christ,
shine forth in the Church
and bring all nations
to the fullness of truth.

Then the bishop sits. The deacon goes to the altar and lights the candles for the celebration of the eucharist.

31. Then the festive lighting takes place: all the candles, including those at the places where the anointings were made, and the other lamps are lit as a sign of rejoicing. Meanwhile the following antiphon is sung with the canticle of Tobias.

Your light will come, Jerusalem; upon you the glory of the Lord will dawn and all nations will walk in your light, alleluia.

Or, during Lent:

Jerusalem, city of God, you will shine with the light of God's splendor; all people on earth will pay you homage.

Canticle of Tobias

(Vg. 13:10; 13-14ab; 14c-15; 17)

Bless the Lord, all you saints of the Lord.
Rejoice and give him thanks.

(Repeat antiphon)

Jerusalem, city of God,
you will shine with the light of God's splendor;
all people on earth will pay you homage.
Nations will come from afar,
bearing gifts for the King of heaven;
in you they will worship the Lord.

(Repeat antiphon)

Nations will consider your land holy,
for in you they will call upon the great name of the Lord.
You will exult and rejoice over the children of the righteous,
for they will be gathered together to praise the Lord.

(Repeat antiphon)

Another appropriate song may be sung, especially one in honor of Christ, the light of the world.

PART IV

LITURGY OF THE EUCHARIST

32. The deacons and the ministers prepare the altar in the usual way. Then some of the congregation bring bread, wine, and water for the celebration of the Lord's sacrifice. The bishop receives the gifts at the chair. While the gifts are being brought, the following antiphon may be sung:

Lord God, in the simplicity of my heart I have joyously offered all things to you; with great joy I have looked upon your chosen people; Lord God, I have obeyed your will (alleluia).

Another appropriate song may be sung.

■ **33.** When all is ready, the bishop goes to the altar, removes the miter, and kisses the altar. The Mass proceeds in the usual way; however, neither the gifts nor the altar are incensed.

Prayer Over the Gifts

■ **34.** With hands extended, the bishop sings or says:

Lord,
accept the gifts of a rejoicing Church.

May your people,
who are gathered in this sacred place,
arrive at eternal salvation
through the mysteries in which they share.

Grant this through Christ our Lord.

R. Amen.

Eucharistic Prayer

■ **35.** Eucharistic Prayer I or III is said, with the following preface. With hands extended the bishop sings or says:

The Lord be with you.

R. And also with you.

Lift up your hearts.

R. We lift them up to the Lord.

Let us give thanks to the Lord our God.

R. It is right to give him thanks and praise.

Father of holiness and power,
we give you thanks and praise
through Jesus Christ, your Son.

▶

For you have blessed this work of our hands
and your presence makes it a house of prayer;
nor do you ever refuse us welcome
when we come in before you as your pilgrim people.

In this house you realize the mystery of your dwelling among us:
for in shaping us here as your holy temple
you enrich your whole Church,
which is the very body of Christ,
and thus bring closer to fulfillment
the vision of your peace,
the heavenly city of Jerusalem.

And so, with all your angels and saints,
who stand in your temple of glory,
we praise you and give you thanks, as we sing:

Holy, holy, holy Lord, God of power and might,
heaven and earth are full of your glory.
  Hosanna in the highest.
Blessed is he who comes in the name of the Lord.
  Hosanna in the highest.

36. While the bishop is receiving the body of Christ the communion song begins. One of the following antiphons is sung with Psalm 128.

> My house shall be called a house of prayer, says the Lord: in it all who ask shall receive, all who seek shall find, and all who knock shall have the door opened to them (alleluia).

> Or:

> May the children of the Church be like olive branches around the table of the Lord (alleluia).

> Another appropriate song may be sung.

> If there is no inauguration of the blessed sacrament chapel, the Mass proceeds as below, no. 38.

Inauguration of the Blessed Sacrament Chapel

■ **37. [79]** The inauguration of a chapel where the blessed sacrament is to be reserved, is carried out appropriately in this way: after the communion the pyx containing the blessed sacrament is left on the table of the altar. The bishop goes to the chair, and all pray in silence for a brief period. Then the bishop says the following prayer after communion:

Let us pray.

Pause for silent prayer, if this has not preceded.

Lord,
through these gifts
increase the vision of your truth in our minds.

May we always worship you in your holy temple,
and rejoice in your presence with all your saints.

Grant this through Christ our Lord.

℟. Amen.

[80] When the prayer is completed, the bishop returns to the altar, genuflects, and incenses the blessed sacrament. Afterward, when he has received the humeral veil, he takes the pyx, which he covers with the veil itself. Then a procession is formed in which, preceded by the crossbearer and with lighted torches and incense, the blessed sacrament is carried through the main body of the church to the chapel of reservation. As the procession proceeds, the following antiphon is sung with Psalm 147:12-20.

Praise the Lord, Jerusalem.

Another appropriate song may be sung.

[81] When the procession comes to the chapel of reservation, the bishop places the pyx on the altar or in the tabernacle, the door of which remains open. Then he puts incense in the censer, kneels, and incenses the blessed sacrament. Finally, after a brief period during which all pray in silence, the deacon puts the pyx in the tabernacle or closes the door. A minister lights the lamp, which will burn perpetually before the blessed sacrament.

[82] If the chapel where the blessed sacrament is reserved can be seen clearly by the congregation, the bishop immediately imparts the blessing of the Mass (see below, no. 39). Otherwise the procession returns to the sanctuary by the shorter route and the bishop imparts the blessing either at the altar or at the chair.

Prayer after Communion

38. If there is no inauguration of the blessed sacrament chapel, when the communion of the congregation is finished, the bishop says:

Let us pray.

Pause for silent prayer, if this has not preceded.

**Lord,
through these gifts
increase the vision of your truth in our minds.**

**May we always worship you in your holy temple,
and rejoice in your presence with all your saints.**

Grant this through Christ our Lord.

R. Amen.

Blessing and Dismissal

■ **39.** The bishop receives the miter and says:

The Lord be with you.

R. And also with you.

Then the deacon, if appropriate, gives the invitation to the people in these or similar words:

Bow your heads and pray for God's blessing.

■ Then the bishop extends his hands over the people and blesses them, saying:

**The Lord of earth and heaven
has assembled you before him this day
to dedicate this house of prayer.
May he fill you with the blessings of heaven.**

R. Amen.

**God the Father wills that all his children
scattered through the world
become one family in his Son.
May he make you his temple,
the dwelling place of his Holy Spirit.**

R. Amen.

May God free you from every bond of sin,
dwell within you and give you joy.
May you live with him for ever
in the company of all his saints.

℟. Amen.

The bishop takes the pastoral staff and continues:

May almighty God bless you,
the Father, and the Son, + and the Holy Spirit.

℟. Amen.

40. Finally the deacon dismisses the people in the usual way.

CHAPTER FOUR

RITE OF DEDICATION OF AN ALTAR

INTRODUCTION

I. NATURE AND DIGNITY OF THE ALTAR

1. From meditating on God's word, the ancient Fathers of the Church did not hesitate to assert that Christ was the victim, priest, and altar of his own sacrifice.[1] For in the Letter to the Hebrews Christ is presented as the High Priest who is also the living altar of the heavenly temple;[2] and in the Book of Revelation our Redeemer appears as the Lamb who has been sacrificed[3] and whose offering is taken by the holy angel to the altar in heaven.[4]

The Christian Is Also a Spiritual Altar

2. Since Christ, Head and Teacher, is the true altar, his members and disciples are also spiritual altars on which the sacrifice of a holy life is offered to God. The Fathers seem to have this in mind. St. Ignatius of Antioch asks the Romans quite plainly: "Grant me only this favor: let my blood be spilled in sacrifice to God, while there is still an altar ready."[5] St. Polycarp exhorts widows to lead a life of holiness, for "they are God's altar."[6] Among others, St. Gregory the Great echoes these words when he says: "What is God's altar if not the souls of those who lead good lives? . . . Rightly, then, the heart of the just is said to be the altar of God."[7]

    In another image frequently used by the writers of the Church, Christians who give themselves to prayer, offer petitions to God, and present sacrifices of supplication, are the living stones out of which the Lord Jesus builds the Church's altar.[8]

The Altar, Table of the Sacrifice and the Paschal Meal

3. By instituting in the form of a sacrificial meal the memorial of the sacrifice he was about to offer the Father on the altar of the cross, Christ made holy the table where the community would

---

[1] See Epiphanius, *Panarium* 2, 1, *Haeresis* 55: PG 41, 979. Cyril of Alexandia, *De adoratione in spiritu et veritate* 9: PG 68, 647.

[2] See Heb 4:14; 13:10.

[3] See Rv 5:6.

[4] See RM, Order of Mass, no. 96.

[5] Ignatius of Antioch, *Ad Romanos* 2:2: Funk PA 1:255.

[6] Polycarp, *Ad Philippenses* 4:3: Funk PA 1:301.

[7] Gregory the Great, *Homiliarum in Ezechielem* 10, 19: PL 76, 1069.

[8] See Origen, *In librum Iesu Nave*, Homilia 9, 1: SC 71, 244 and 246.

come to celebrate their Passover. Therefore the altar is the table for a sacrifice and for a banquet. At this table the priest, representing Christ the Lord, accomplishes what the Lord himself did and what he handed on to his disciples to do in his memory. The Apostle clearly intimates this: "The blessing cup that we bless is a communion with the blood of Christ and the bread that we break is a communion with the body of Christ. The fact that there is only one loaf means that though there are many of us, we form a single Body because we all have a share in this one loaf."[9]

The Altar, Sign of Christ

4.   The Church's children have the power to celebrate the memorial of Christ and take their place at the Lord's table anywhere that circumstances might require. But it is in keeping with the eucharistic mystery that the Christian people erect a permanent altar for the celebration of the Lord's Supper and they have done so from the earliest times.

The Christian altar is by its very nature properly the table of sacrifice and of the paschal banquet. It is:

— a unique altar on which the sacrifice of the cross is perpetuated in mystery throughout the ages until Christ comes;

— a table at which the Church's children gather to give thanks to God and receive the body and blood of Christ.

In every church, then, the altar "is the center of the thanksgiving that the eucharist accomplishes"[10] and around which the Church's other rites are, in a certain manner, arrayed.[11]

At the altar the memorial of the Lord is celebrated and his body and blood given to the people. Therefore the Church's writers have seen in the altar a sign of Christ himself. This is the basis for the saying: "The altar is Christ."

The Altar as Honoring Martyrs

5.   All the dignity of the altar rests on its being the Lord's table. Thus the martyr's body does not bring honor to the altar; rather the altar does honor to the martyr's tomb. For it is altogether proper to erect altars over the burial place of martyrs and other saints or to deposit their relics beneath altars as a mark of respect and as a symbol of the truth that the sacrifice of the members has its source in the sacrifice of the Head.[12] Thus "the triumphant victims come to their rest in the place where Christ is victim: he, however, who suffered for all is on the altar; they who have been

[9] See 1 Cor 10:16-17.
[10] GIRM, no. 259.
[11] See Pius XII, Encycl. *Mediator Dei*: AAS 39 (1947) 529.
[12] See RM, Common of Martyrs 8, prayer over the gifts.
[13] Ambrose, *Epistula* 22, 13: PL 16, 1023. See Ps. Maximus of Turin, *Sermo* 78: PL 57, 689-690.

redeemed by his sufferings are beneath the altar."[13] This arrangement would seem to recall in a certain manner the spiritual vision of the Apostle John in the Book of Revelation: "I saw underneath the altar the souls of all the people who have been killed on account of the word of God, for witnessing to it."[14] His meaning is that although all the saints are rightly called Christ's witnesses, the witness of blood has a special significance that only the relics of the martyrs beneath the altar express in its entirety.

II. ERECTING AN ALTAR

6. It is desirable that in every church there be a fixed altar and that in other places set apart for sacred celebrations there be either a fixed or a movable altar.

A fixed altar is one so constructed that it is attached to the floor so that it cannot be moved; a movable altar can be transferred from place to place.[15]

7. In new churches it is better to erect only one altar so that in the one assembly of the people of God the single altar signifies the one Savior Jesus Christ and the one eucharist of the Church.

But an altar may also be erected in a chapel (somewhat separated, if possible, from the body of the church) where the tabernacle for the reservation of the blessed sacrament is situated. On weekdays when there is a small gathering of people Mass may be celebrated at this altar.

The merely decorative erection of several altars in a church must be entirely avoided.

8. The altar should be freestanding so that the priest can easily walk around it and celebrate Mass facing the people. "It should be so placed as to be a focal point on which the attention of the whole congregation centers naturally."[16]

9. In accordance with received custom in the Church and the biblical symbolism connected with an altar, the table of a fixed altar should be of stone, indeed of natural stone. But, at the discretion of the conference of bishops, any becoming, solid, and finely wrought material may be used in erecting an altar.

The pedestal or base of the table may be of any sort of material, provided it is becoming and solid.[17]

10. The altar is of its very nature dedicated to the one God, for the eucharistic sacrifice is offered to the one God. This is the sense in which the Church's practice of dedicating altars to God in

[14] Rv 6:9.
[15] See GIRM, nos. 265, 261.
[16] GIRM, no. 262.
[17] See GIRM, no. 263.

honor of the saints must be understood. St. Augustine expresses it well: "It is not to any of the martyrs, but to the God of the martyrs, though in memory of the martyrs, that we raise our altars."[18]

This should be made clear to the people. In new churches statues and pictures of saints may not be placed above the altar.

Likewise, when relics of saints are exposed for veneration, they should not be placed on the table of the altar.

11. It is fitting to continue the tradition in the Roman liturgy of placing relics of martyrs or other saints beneath the altar.[19] But the following should be noted.

a) Such relics should be of a size sufficient for them to be recognizable as parts of human bodies. Hence excessively small relics of one or more saints must not be placed beneath an altar.

b) The greatest care must be taken to determine whether the relics in question are authentic. It is better for an altar to be dedicated without relics than to have relics of doubtful authenticity placed beneath it.

c) A reliquary must not be placed on the altar or set into the table of the altar, but placed beneath the table of the altar, as the design of the altar permits.

When the rite of depositing relics takes place, it is highly recommended to keep a vigil at the relics of the martyr or saint, in accordance with the provisions of chapter two, no. 10.

III. CELEBRATION OF THE DEDICATION

Minister of the Rite

12. Since the bishop has been entrusted with the care of the particular Church, it is his responsibility to dedicate to God new altars built in his diocese.

If he cannot himself preside at the rite, he shall entrust the function to another bishop, especially to one who is his associate and assistant in the pastoral care of the community for which the new altar has been erected or, in altogether special circumstances, to a priest, to whom he shall give a special mandate.

Choice of Day

13. Since an altar becomes sacred principally by the celebration of the eucharist, in fidelity to this truth the celebration of Mass on a new altar before it has been dedicated is to be carefully avoided, so that the Mass of dedication may also be the first eucharist celebrated on the altar.

---

[18] Augustine, *Contra Faustum* 20, 21: PL 42, 384.
[19] See GIRM, no. 266.

14. A day should be chosen for the dedication of a new altar when the people can be present in large numbers, especially a Sunday, unless pastoral considerations suggest otherwise. However, the rite of the dedication of an altar may not be celebrated during the Easter triduum, on Ash Wednesday, the weekdays of Holy Week, and All Souls.

Mass of the Dedication

15. The celebration of the eucharist is inseparably bound up with the rite of the dedication of an altar. The Mass is the Mass for the dedication of an altar. On Christmas, Epiphany, Ascension, Pentecost, and on the Sundays of Advent, Lent, and the Easter season, the Mass is the Mass of the day, with the exception of the prayer over the gifts and the preface, which are closely interwoven with the rite itself.

16. It is fitting that the bishop concelebrate the Mass with the priests present, especially with those who have been given charge over the parish or the community for which the altar has been erected.

Parts of the Rite

A. Introductory Rites

17. The introductory rites of the Mass of the dedication of an altar take place in the usual way except that in place of the penitential rite the bishop blesses water and with it sprinkles the people and the new altar.

B. Liturgy of the Word

18. It is commendable to have three readings in the liturgy of the word, chosen, according to the rubrical norm, either from the liturgy of the day (see no. 15) or from those in the Lectionary for the rite of the dedication of an altar (nos. 704 and 706).

19. After the readings, the bishop gives the homily, in which he explains the biblical readings and the meaning of the dedication of an altar.

After the homily, the profession of faith is said. The general intercessions are omitted, since the Litany of the Saints is sung in their place.

C. Prayer of Dedication and the Anointing of the Altar

Depositing of the Relics of the Saints

20. If it is to take place, the relics of martyrs or other saints are placed beneath the altar after the Litany of the Saints. The rite is meant to signify that all who have been baptized in the death of Christ, especially those who have shed their blood for the Lord, share in Christ's passion (see no. 5).

Prayer of Dedication

21. The celebration of the eucharist is the most important and the one necessary rite for the dedication of an altar. Nevertheless, in accordance with the universal tradition of the Church in both East and West, a special prayer of dedication is also said. This prayer is a sign of the intention to dedicate the altar to the Lord for all times and a petition for his blessing.

Rites of Anointing, Incensing, Covering, and Lighting the Altar

22. The rites of anointing, incensing, covering, and lighting the altar express in visible signs several aspects of the invisible work that the Lord accomplishes through the Church in its celebration of the divine mysteries, especially the eucharist.

a) *Anointing* of the altar: The anointing with chrism makes the altar a symbol of Christ, who, before all others, is and is called "The Anointed One"; for the Father anointed him with the Holy Spirit and constituted him the High Priest so that on the altar of his body he might offer the sacrifice of his life for the salvation of all.

b) *Incense* is burned on the altar to signify that Christ's sacrifice, there perpetuated in mystery, ascends to God as an odor of sweetness, and also to signify that the people's prayers rise up pleasing and acceptable, reaching the throne of God.[20]

c) *The covering of the altar* indicates that the Christian altar is the altar of the eucharistic sacrifice and the table of the Lord; around it priests and people, by one and the same rite but with a difference of function, celebrate the memorial of Christ's death and resurrection and partake of his supper. For this reason the altar is prepared as the table of the sacrificial banquet and adorned as for a feast. Thus the dressing of the altar clearly signifies that it is the Lord's table at which all God's people joyously meet to be refreshed with divine food, namely, the body and blood of Christ sacrificed.

d) *The lighting of the altar* teaches us that Christ is "a light to enlighten the nations";[21] his brightness shines out in the Church and through it in the whole human family.

---

[20] See Rv 8:3-4: An angel "who had a golden censer, came and stood at the altar. A large quantity of incense was given to him to offer with the prayers of all the saints on the golden altar that stood in front of the throne; and so from the angel's hand the smoke of the incense went up in the presence of God and with it the prayers of the saints."

[21] Lk 2:32.

D. Celebration of the Eucharist

23. After the altar has been prepared, the bishop celebrates the eucharist, the principal and the most ancient part of the whole rite,[22] because the celebration of the eucharist is in the closest harmony with the rite of the dedication of an altar:

— For the celebration of the eucharistic sacrifice achieves the end for which the altar was erected and expresses this end by particularly clear signs.

— Furthermore, the eucharist, which sanctifies the hearts of those who receive it, in a sense consecrates the altar, as the ancient Fathers of the Church often assert: "This altar should be an object of awe: by nature it is stone, but it is made holy when it receives the body of Christ."[23]

— Finally, the bond closely connecting the dedication of an altar with the celebration of the eucharist is likewise evident from the fact that the Mass for the dedication has its own preface, which is a central part of the rite itself.

IV. ADAPTATION OF THE RITE

Adaptations within the Competence of the Conferences of Bishops

24. The conferences of bishops may adapt this rite, as required, to the character of each region, but in such a way that nothing of its dignity and solemnity is lost.

However, the following are to be respected:

a) The celebration of Mass with the proper preface and prayer for a dedication must never be omitted.

b) Rites that have a special meaning and force from liturgical tradition (see no. 22) must be retained, unless weighty reasons stand in the way, but the wording may be suitably adapted if necessary.

With regard to adaptations, the competent ecclesiastical authority is to consult the Holy See and introduce adaptations with its consent.[24]

Adaptations within the Competence of the Ministers

25. It is for the bishop and for those in charge of the celebration of the rite to decide whether to have the depositing of relics of the saints; in so doing, they are to follow what is laid down in

---

[22] See Pope Vigilius, *Epistula ad Profuturum Episcopum* 4: PL 84, 832.
[23] John Chrysostom, *Homilia 20 in 2 Cor 3*: PG 61, 540.
[24] See SC, art. 40.

no. 11 and they are to take as the decisive consideration the spiritual good of the community and a proper sense of liturgy.

It is for the rector of the church in which the altar is to be dedicated, helped by those who assist him in the pastoral work, to decide and prepare everything concerning the readings, singing, and other pastoral aids to foster the fruitful participation of the people and to ensure a dignified celebration.

V. Pastoral Preparation

26. The people are to be informed in good time about the dedication of a new altar and they are to be properly prepared to take an active part in the rite. Accordingly, they should be taught what each rite means and how it is carried out. For the purpose of giving this instruction, use may be made of what has been said earlier about the nature and dignity of an altar and the meaning and import of the rites. In this way the people will be imbued with the rightful love that is owed to the altar.

VI. Requisites for the Dedication of an Altar

27. For the celebration of the rite the following should be prepared:
    — The Roman Missal;

    — The Lectionary;

    — The Roman Pontifical;

    — the cross and the Book of the Gospels to be carried in the procession;

    — container of water to be blessed and sprinkler;

    — container with the holy chrism;

    — towels for wiping the table of the altar;

    — if needed, a waxen linen cloth or waterproof covering of the same size as the altar;

    — basin and jug of water, towels, and all that is needed for washing the bishop's hands;

    — linen gremial;

    — brazier for burning incense or aromatic spices; or grains of incense and small candles to burn on the altar;

    — censer, incense boat and spoon;

    — chalice, corporal, purificators, and hand towel;

    — bread, wine, and water for the celebration of Mass;

    — altar cross, unless there is already a cross in the sanctuary, or the cross that is carried in the entrance procession is to be placed near the altar;

— altar cloth, candles, and candlesticks;

— flowers, if opportune.

28. For the Mass of the dedication the vestments are white or of some festive color. The following should be prepared:

— for the bishop: alb, stole, chasuble, miter, pastoral staff, and pallium, if the bishop has the right to wear one;

— for the concelebrating priests: the vestments for concelebrating Mass;

— for the deacons: albs, stoles, and dalmatics;

— for other ministers: albs or other lawfully approved dress.

29. If relics of the saints are to be placed beneath the altar, the following should be prepared:

a) *In the place from which the procession begins:*

— a reliquary containing the relics, placed between flowers and lights. But as circumstances dictate, the reliquary may be placed in a suitable part of the sanctuary before the rite begins;

— for the deacons who will carry the relics to be deposited: albs, red stoles, if the relics are those of a martyr, or white in other cases, and, if available, dalmatics. If the relics are carried by priests, then, in place of dalmatics, chasubles should be prepared. Relics may also be carried by other ministers, vested in albs or other lawfully approved dress.

b) *In the sanctuary:*

— a small table on which the reliquary is placed during the first part of the dedication rite.

c) *In the sacristy:*

— a sealant or cement to close the cover of the aperture. In addition, a stonemason should be on hand to close the depository of the relics at the proper time.

30. It is fitting to observe the custom of enclosing in the reliquary a parchment on which is recorded the day, month, and year of the dedication of the altar, the name of the bishop who celebrated the rite, the titular of the church, and the names of the martyrs or saints whose relics are deposited beneath the altar.

A record of the dedication of the church is to be drawn up in duplicate and signed by the bishop, the rector of the church, and representatives of the local community; one copy is to be kept in the diocesan archives, the other in the archives of the church.

OUTLINE OF THE RITE

INTRODUCTORY RITES
Entrance into the Church
    Entrance Procession
    Greeting
Blessing and Sprinkling of Water
Hymn: Gloria
Opening Prayer

LITURGY OF THE WORD
First Reading
Responsorial Psalm
Second Reading
Gospel Acclamation
Gospel
Homily
Profession of Faith

PRAYER OF DEDICATION AND THE ANOINTINGS
Invitation to Prayer
Litany of the Saints
Concluding Prayer
[Depositing of the Relics]
Prayer of Dedication
Anointing of the Altar
Incensation of the Altar
Lighting of the Altar

LITURGY OF THE EUCHARIST
Preparation of the Altar and the Gifts
Prayer over the Gifts
Eucharistic Prayer

Communion
Prayer after Communion

CONCLUDING RITE
Blessing and Dismissal

RITE OF DEDICATION

PART I

INTRODUCTORY RITES

Entrance into the Church

31. When the people are assembled, the bishop and the concelebrating priests, the deacons, and the ministers, each in appropriate vestments, preceded by the crossbearer, go from the sacristy through the main body of the church to the sanctuary.

32. If there are relics of the saints to be placed beneath the altar, these are brought in the entrance procession to the sanctuary from the sacristy or the chapel where since the vigil they have been exposed for the veneration of the people. For a just cause, before the celebration begins, the relics may be placed between lighted torches in a suitable part of the sanctuary.

33. As the procession proceeds, the entrance antiphon is sung with Psalm 43.

O God, our shield, look with favor on the face of your anointed; one day within your courts is better than a thousand elsewhere (alleluia).

Or:

I will go to the altar of God, the God of my joy.

Another appropriate song may be sung.

34. When the procession reaches the sanctuary, the relics of the saints are placed between lighted torches in a suitable place. The concelebrating priests, the deacons, and the ministers go to the places assigned to them; the bishop, without kissing the altar, goes to the chair. Then, putting aside the pastoral staff and miter, he greets the people, saying:

The grace and peace of God
be with all of you
in his holy Church.

R. And also with you.

Other suitable words taken preferably from sacred Scripture may be used.

Blessing and Sprinkling of Water

■ **35.** When the entrance rite is completed, the bishop blesses water with which to sprinkle the people as a sign of repentance and as a reminder of their baptism, and to purify the altar. The ministers bring the vessel with the water to the bishop who stands at the chair. The bishop invites all to pray, in these or similar words:

Brothers and sisters in Christ, this is a day of rejoicing: we have come together to dedicate this altar by offering the sacrifice of Christ.

May we respond to these holy rites, receive God's word with faith, share at the Lord's table with joy, and raise our hearts in hope.

Gathered around this one altar we draw nearer to Christ, the living stone, in whom we become God's holy temple.

But first let us ask God to bless this gift of water. As it is sprinkled upon us and upon this altar, may it be a sign of our repentance and a reminder of our baptism.

All pray in silence for a brief period. The bishop then continues:

God of mercy,
you call every creature to the light of life,
and surround us with such great love
that when we stray
you continually lead us back to Christ our head.

For you have established an inheritance of such mercy,
that those sinners, who pass through water made sacred,
die with Christ to rise restored
as members of his body
and heirs of his eternal covenant.

Bless + this water;
sanctify it.

As it is sprinkled upon us and upon this altar
make it a sign of the saving waters of baptism,
by which we become one in Christ, the temple of your Spirit.

May all here today,
and all those in days to come,
who will celebrate your mysteries on this altar,
be united at last in the holy city of your peace.

We ask this in the name of Jesus the Lord.

R. Amen.

■ **36.** When the invocation over the water is finished, the bishop, accompanied by the deacons, passes through the main body of the church, sprinkling the people with the holy water; then, when he has returned to the sanctuary, he sprinkles the altar. Meanwhile the following antiphon is sung.

> I saw water flowing from the right side of the temple, alleluia. It brought God's life and his salvation, and the people sang in joyful praise: alleluia, alleluia.

> Or, during Lent:

> I will pour clean water over you and wash away all your defilement. A new heart will I give you, says the Lord.

> Another appropriate song may be sung.

■ **37.** After the sprinkling the bishop returns to the chair and, when the singing is finished, standing with hands joined, says:

May God, the Father of mercies,
to whom we dedicate this altar on earth,
forgive us our sins
and enable us to offer
an unending sacrifice of praise
on his altar in heaven.

R. Amen.

Hymn

38. Then the **Gloria** is sung.

Opening Prayer

■ **39.** When the hymn is finished, the bishop, with hands joined, says:

Let us pray.

> All pray in silence for a brief period. Then the bishop, with hands extended, says:

Lord,
you willed that all things be drawn to your Son,
mounted on the altar of the cross.

▶

Bless those who dedicate this altar to your service.

May it be the table of our unity,
a banquet of plenty,
and a source of the Spirit,
in whom we grow daily as your faithful people.

We ask this through our Lord Jesus Christ, your Son,
who lives and reigns with you and the Holy Spirit,
one God, for ever and ever.

℞. Amen.

PART II

LITURGY OF THE WORD

40. In the liturgy of the word everything takes place in the usual way. The readings and the gospel are taken, in accordance with the rubrics, either from the texts in *The Lectionary* (nos. 704 and 706) for the rite of the dedication of an altar or from the Mass of the day.

41. After the gospel the bishop gives the homily, in which he explains the biblical readings and the meaning of the rite.

42. The profession of faith is said. The general intercessions are omitted since in their place the litany of the saints is sung.

PART III

PRAYER OF DEDICATION AND THE ANOINTINGS

Invitation to Prayer

43. Then all stand, and the bishop, without his miter, invites the people to pray in these or similar words:

Let our prayers go forth to God the Father through Jesus Christ, his Son, with whom are joined all the saints who have shared in his suffering and now sit at his table of glory.

Deacon (except on Sundays and during the Easter season):

Let us kneel.

Litany of the Saints

44. Then the litany of the saints is sung, with all responding. On Sundays and also during the Easter season, all stand; on other days, all kneel.

45. The cantors begin the litany (appendix, p. 104); they add, at the proper place, names of other saints (the titular of the church, the patron saint of the place, and the saints whose relics are to be deposited, if this is to take place) and petitions suitable to the occasion.

■ **46.** When the litany is finished, the bishop, standing with hands extended, says:

Lord,
may the prayers of the Blessed Virgin Mary
and of all the saints
make our prayers acceptable to you.

May this altar be the place
where the great mysteries of redemption are accomplished:
a place where your people offer their gifts,
unfold their good intentions,
pour out their prayers,
and echo every meaning of their faith and devotion.

Grant this through Christ our Lord.

℟. Amen.

If it is applicable, the deacon says:

Let us stand.

All rise. The bishop receives the miter.

When there is no depositing of the relics of the saints, the bishop immediately says the prayer of dedication as indicated in no. 48 below.

Depositing of the Relics

■ **47.** Then, if relics of the martyrs or other saints are to be placed beneath the altar, the bishop approaches the altar. A deacon or priest brings them to the bishop, who places them in a suitably prepared aperture. Meanwhile one of the following antiphons is sung with Psalm 15.

> Saints of God, you have been enthroned at the foot of God's altar; pray for us to the Lord Jesus Christ.

Or:

> The bodies of the saints lie buried in peace, but their names will live on for ever (alleluia).

Another appropriate song may be sung.

Meanwhile a stone mason closes the aperture and the bishop returns to the chair.

Prayer of Dedication

■ **48.** Then the bishop, standing without miter at the chair or near the altar, with hands extended, says:

Father,
we praise you and give you thanks,
for you have established the sacrament of true worship
by bringing to perfection in Christ
the mystery of the one true altar
prefigured in those many altars of old.

Noah,
the second father of the human race,
once the waters fell and the mountains peaked again,
built an altar in your name.
You, Lord, were appeased by his fragrant offering
and your rainbow bore witness
to a covenant refounded in love.

Abraham,
our father in faith,
wholeheartedly accepted your word
and constructed an altar on which to slay
Isaac, his only son.
But you, Lord, stayed his hand
and provided a ram for his offering.

Moses,
mediator of the old law,

built an altar
on which was cast the blood of a lamb:
so prefiguring the altar of the cross.

All this Christ has fulfilled in the paschal mystery:
as priest and victim he freely mounted the tree of the cross
and gave himself to you, Father, as the one perfect oblation.
In his sacrifice the new covenant is sealed,
in his blood sin is engulfed.

Lord, we therefore stand before you in prayer.

Bless this altar built in the house of the Church,
that it may ever be reserved for the sacrifice of Christ,
and stand for ever as the Lord's table,
where your people will find nourishment and strength.

Make this altar a sign of Christ
from whose pierced side flowed blood and water,
which ushered in the sacraments of the Church.

Make it a table of joy,
where the friends of Christ may hasten
to cast upon you their burdens and cares
and take up their journey restored.

Make it a place of communion and peace,
so that those who share the body and blood of your Son
may be filled with his Spirit
and grow in your life of love.

Make it a source of unity and friendship,
where your people may gather as one
to share your spirit of mutual love.

Make it the center of our praise and thanksgiving
until we arrive at the eternal tabernacle,
where, together with Christ,
high priest and living altar,
we will offer you an everlasting sacrifice of praise.

We ask this through our Lord Jesus Christ, your Son,
who lives and reigns with you and the Holy Spirit,
one God, for ever and ever.

R. Amen.

Anointing of the Altar

■ **49.** When the above is finished, the bishop, removing the chasuble if necessary and putting on a linen gremial, goes to the altar with the deacon or another minister, one of whom carries the chrism. Standing before the altar, the bishop says:

We now anoint this altar.
May God in his power make it holy,
a visible sign of the mystery of Christ,
who offered himself for the life of the world.

Then he pours chrism on the middle of the altar and on each of its four corners, and it is recommended that he anoint the entire table of the altar with this.

50. During the anointing, outside the Easter Season, the following antiphon is sung (see below, no. 51) with Psalm 45.

God, your God, has anointed you with the oil of gladness.

Another appropriate song may be sung.

51. During the Easter Season the following antiphon is sung with Psalm 118.

The stone which the builders rejected has become the keystone of the building, alleluia.

Another appropriate song may be sung.

■ **52.** When the altar has been anointed, the bishop returns to the chair, sits, and washes his hands. Then the bishop takes off the gremial and puts on the chasuble.

Incensation of the Altar

■ **53.** After the rite of annointing, a brazier is placed on the altar for burning incense or aromatic gums, or, if desired, a heap of incense mixed with small candles or wax tapers is made on the altar. The bishop puts incense into the brazier or he lights the heap of incense with a small candle handed to him by a minister, saying:

Lord,
may our prayer ascend as incense in your sight.
As this building is filled with fragrance
so may your Church fill the world
with the fragrance of Christ.

Then the bishop puts incense into the censer and incenses the altar; he returns to the chair, is incensed, and then sits. A minister incenses the people. Meanwhile one of the following antiphons is sung with Psalm 138.

> **An angel stood by the altar of the temple, holding a golden censer.**

Or:

> **From the hand of the angel, clouds of incense rose in the presence of the Lord.**

Another appropriate song may be sung.

Lighting of the Altar

54. After the incensation, a few ministers wipe the table of the altar with cloths, and, if need be, cover it with a waterproof linen. They then cover the altar with a cloth, and, if opportune, decorate it with flowers. They arrange in a suitable manner the candles needed for the celebration of Mass, and, if need be, the cross.

55. Then the bishop gives to the deacon a lighted candle, and says:

**Light of Christ,
shine on this altar
and be reflected by those
who share at this table.**

Then the bishop sits. The deacon goes to the altar and lights the candles for the celebration of the eucharist.

56. Then the festive lighting takes place: as a sign of rejoicing all the lamps around the altar are lit. Meanwhile the following antiphon is sung.

> **In you, O Lord, is the fountain of life; in your light we shall see light.**

Another appropriate song may be sung, especially one in honor of Christ, the light of the world.

PART IV

LITURGY OF THE EUCHARIST

57. The deacons and the ministers prepare the altar in the usual way. Then some of the congregation bring bread. wine, and water for the celebration of the Lord's sacrifice. The bishop receives the gifts at the chair. While the gifts are being brought, one of the following antiphons may be sung.

If you are bringing your gift to the altar, and there you remember that your neighbor has something against you, leave your gift in front of the altar; go at once and make peace with your neighbor, and then come back and offer your gift, alleluia.

Or:

Moses consecrated the altar to the Lord and offered sacrifices and burnt offerings; he made an evening sacrifice of sweet fragrance to the Lord God in the sight of the children of Israel.

Another appropriate song may be sung.

■ **58.** When all is ready, the bishop goes to the altar, removes the miter, and kisses the altar. The Mass proceeds in the usual way; however, neither the gifts nor the altar are incensed.

Prayer Over the Gifts

■ **59.** With hands extended, the bishop sings or says:

Lord,
send your Spirit upon this altar
to sanctify these gifts;
may he prepare our hearts
to receive them worthily.

Grant this through Christ our Lord.

℟. Amen.

Eucharistic Prayer

■ **60.** Eucharistic Prayer I or III is said, with the following preface, which is an integral part of the rite of the dedication of an altar:

The Lord be with you.

℟. And also with you

Lift up your hearts.

℟. We lift them up to the Lord.

Let us give thanks to the Lord our God.

℟. It is right to give him thanks and praise.

Father, all-powerful and ever-living God,
we do well always and everywhere to give you thanks
through Jesus Christ our Lord.

True priest and true victim,
he offered himself to you
on the altar of the cross
and commanded us to celebrate
that same sacrifice,
until he comes again.

Therefore your people have built this altar
and have dedicated it to your name
with grateful hearts.

This is a truly sacred place.

Here the sacrifice of Christ is offered in mystery,
perfect praise is given to you,
and our redemption is made continually present.

Here is prepared the Lord's table,
at which your children,
nourished by the body of Christ,
are gathered into a Church, one and holy.

Here your people drink of the Spirit,
the stream of living water,
flowing from the rock of Christ.
They will become, in him,
a worthy offering and a living altar.

We praise you, Lord,
with all the angels and saints in their song of joy:

Holy, holy, holy Lord, God of power and might,
heaven and earth are full of your glory.
    Hosanna in the highest.
Blessed is he who comes in the name of the Lord.
    Hosanna in the highest.

61. While the bishop is receiving the body of Christ the communion song begins. One of the following antiphons is sung with Psalm 128.

Even the sparrow finds a home and the swallow a nest wherein she places her young: near to your altars, O Lord of Hosts, my King and my God.

Or:

May the children of the Church be like olive branches around the table of the Lord (alleluia).

Another appropriate song may be sung.

Prayer After Communion

■ **62.** Then, standing at the chair or at the altar, the bishop sings or says:

Let us pray.

Pause for silent prayer, if this has not preceded.

Lord,
may we always be drawn
to this altar of sacrifice.

United in faith and love,
may we be nourished by the body of Christ
and transformed into his likeness,
who lives and reigns with you and the Holy Spirit,
one God, for ever and ever.

R. Amen.

Blessing and Dismissal

■ **63.** The bishop receives the miter and says:

The Lord be with you.

R. And also with you.

Then the deacon, if appropriate, gives the invitation to the people in these or similar words:

Bow your heads and pray for God's blessing.

■   Then the bishop extends his hands over the people and blesses them, saying:

May God, who has given you the dignity
of a royal priesthood,
strengthen you in your holy service
and make you worthy to share in his sacrifice.
R. Amen.

May he, who invites you to the one table
and feeds you with the one bread,
make you one in heart and mind.
R. Amen.

May all to whom you proclaim Christ
be drawn to him
by the example of your love.
R. Amen.

The bishop takes the pastoral staff and continues:

May almighty God bless you,
the Father, and the Son, + and the Holy Spirit.
R. Amen.

64.   Finally the deacon dismisses the people in the usual way.

CHAPTER FIVE

RITE OF BLESSING A CHURCH

INTRODUCTION

1.   Since sacred edifices, that is, churches, are permanently set aside for the celebration of the divine mysteries, it is right for them to receive a dedication to God. This is done according to the rite in chapters two and three for dedicating a church, a rite impressive for its striking ceremonies and symbols.

Oratories, chapels, or other sacred edifices set aside only temporarily for divine worship because of special conditions, more properly receive a blessing, according to the rite described below.

2.   As to the structure of the liturgy, the choice of a titular, and the pastoral preparation of the people, what is said in the Introduction to chapter two, nos. 4-5, 7, 20, is to be followed, with the necessary modifications.

A church or an oratory is blessed by the bishop of the diocese or by a priest delegated by him.

3.   A church or an oratory may be blessed on any day, apart from the Easter triduum. As far as possible a day should be chosen when the people can be present in large numbers, especially a Sunday, unless pastoral considerations suggest otherwise.

4.   On days mentioned in the Table of Liturgical Days, nos. 1-4, the Mass is the Mass of the day; but on other days the Mass is either the Mass of the day or the Mass of the titular of the church or oratory.

5.   For the rite of the blessing of a church or an oratory all things needed for the celebration of Mass are prepared. But even though it may have already been blessed or dedicated, the altar should be left bare until the beginning of the liturgy of the eucharist. In a suitable place in the sanctuary the following also should be prepared:

— container of water to be blessed and sprinkler;

— censer, incense boat and spoon;

— The Roman Pontifical;

— altar cross, unless there is already a cross in the sanctuary, or the cross that is carried in the entrance procession is to be placed near the altar;

— altar cloth, candles, candlesticks, and flowers, if opportune.

6.   When at the same time as the church is blessed the altar is to be consecrated, all those things should be prepared that are listed in chapter four, no. 27 and no. 29, if relics of the saints are to be deposited beneath the altar.

7.   For the Mass of the blessing of a church the vestments are white or some festive color. The following should be prepared:

— for the bishop: alb, stole, chasuble, miter, pastoral staff;

— for a priest: the vestments for celebrating Mass;

— for the concelebrating priests: the vestments for concelebrating Mass;

— for the deacons: albs, stoles, and dalmatics;

— for other ministers: albs or other lawfully approved dress.

OUTLINE OF THE RITE

INTRODUCTORY RITES
Entrance into the Church
Greeting
Blessing and Sprinkling of Water
Hymn: Gloria
Opening Prayer

LITURGY OF THE WORD
First Reading
Responsorial Psalm
Second Reading
Gospel Acclamation
Gospel
Homily
[Profession of Faith]

BLESSING OF THE ALTAR
Prayer of Blessing
Incensation of the Altar and People

LITURGY OF THE EUCHARIST
Preparation of the Altar
Presentation of the Gifts
Eucharistic Prayer

Communion
[Inauguration of the Blessed Sacrament Chapel]
Prayer after Communion

CONCLUDING RITE
Blessing and Dismissal

RITE OF BLESSING

PART I

INTRODUCTORY RITES

Entrance into the Church

8. When the people are assembled, while the entrance song is being sung, the bishop and the concelebrating priests, the deacons, and the ministers, each in appropriate vestments, preceded by the crossbearer, go from the sacristy through the main body of the church to the sanctuary.

When the procession arrives at the sanctuary, the bishop without kissing or incensing the altar, goes immediately to the chair; the others go to the places assigned to them.

9. The bishop puts aside the pastoral staff and miter, and when the singing is finished, he greets the people, saying:

**The grace and peace of God
be with all of you
in his holy Church.**

R̥. And also with you.

Other suitable words taken preferably from sacred Scripture may be used.

Blessing and Sprinkling of Water

10. Then the bishop blesses water with which to sprinkle the people as a sign of repentance and as a reminder of their baptism, and to purify the walls of the new church or oratory. The ministers bring the vessel with the water to the bishop who stands at the chair. The bishop invites all to pray, in these or similar words:

Brothers and sisters in Christ, this is a day of rejoicing. For we have come together to offer this new church to God.

We ask that he bless us with his grace and, by his power, bless this gift of water. ▶

As it is sprinkled upon us and throughout this new church, may it become a sign of our repentance, a reminder of our baptism, and a symbol of the cleansing of these walls.

But first let us call to mind that we ourselves, who are bound here in faith and love, are the living Church, set in the world, as a sign and witness of God's love for all.

■ **11.** All pray in silence for a brief period. The bishop then continues:

God of mercy,
you call every creature to the light of life,
and surround us with such great love
that when we stray
you continually lead us back to Christ our head.

For you have established an inheritance of such mercy,
that those sinners, who pass through water made sacred,
die with Christ and rise restored
as members of his body
and heirs of his eternal covenant.

Bless + this water;
sanctify it.

As it is sprinkled upon us and throughout this church
make it a sign of the saving waters of baptism,
by which we become one in Christ, the temple of your Spirit.

May all here today,
and all those in days to come,
who will celebrate your mysteries in this church,
be united at last in the holy city of your peace.

We ask this in the name of Jesus the Lord.

℞. Amen.

■ **12.** When the invocation over the water is finished, the bishop, accompanied by the deacons, passes through the main body of the church, sprinkling the people and the walls with the holy water; then, when he has returned to the sanctuary, he sprinkles the altar, unless it is already blessed or dedicated (see above, no. 5). Meanwhile the following antiphon is sung.

> I saw water flowing from the right side of the temple, alleluia. It brought God's life and his salvation, and the people sang in joyful praise: alleluia, alleluia.

Or, during Lent:

I will pour clean water over you and wash away all your defilement. A new heart will I give you, says the Lord.

Another appropriate song may be sung.

■ **13.** After the sprinkling the bishop returns to the chair and, when the singing is finished, standing with hands joined, says:

May God, the Father of mercies,
dwell in this house of prayer.
May the grace of the Holy Spirit cleanse us,
for we are the temple of his presence.

℟. Amen.

Hymn

14. Then, except on Sundays or weekdays of Advent and Lent, the **Gloria** is sung.

Opening Prayer

■ **15.** When the hymn is finished, the following prayer is said except on the days listed in the Table of Liturgical Days, nos. 1-4, when the prayer of the day is used. The bishop, with hands joined, says:

Let us pray.

All pray in silence for a brief period. Then the bishop, with hands extended, says:

Lord,
bless this church,
which we have been privileged to build with your help.

May all who gather here in faith
to listen to your word
and celebrate your sacraments,
experience the presence of Christ,
who promised to be with those
gathered in his name,
for he lives and reigns with you and the Holy Spirit,
one God, for ever and ever.

℟. Amen.

PART II

LITURGY OF THE WORD

16. The readings are taken, in accordance with the rubrics (see above no. 4), either from the texts in *The Lectionary* (nos. 704 and 706) for the rite of the dedication of a church or from the Mass of the day.

17. Neither lights nor incense are carried at the gospel.

18. After the gospel the bishop gives the homily, in which he explains the biblical readings and the meaning of the rite.

19. The profession of faith and the general intercessions are said in the usual way.

PART III

BLESSING OF THE ALTAR

20. Then the bishop goes to bless the altar. Meanwhile the following antiphon is sung.

May the children of the Church be like olive branches around the table of the Lord (alleluia).

Another appropriate song may be sung.

21. When the singing is finished, the bishop, standing without miter, speaks to the people in these or similar words:

Brothers and sisters, our community rejoices as it comes together to bless this altar. Let us ask God to look kindly on the Church's offering placed upon it and to receive his people as an everlasting gift.

All pray in silence for a brief period. Then the bishop, with hands extended, says:

**Blessed are you, Lord our God,
who accepted the sacrifice of Christ,
offered on the altar of the cross
for the salvation of the world.**

Now with a Father's love,
you call your people to celebrate his memory
by coming together at his table.

May this altar,
which we have built for your holy mysteries,
be the center of our praise and thanksgiving.

May it be the table
at which we break the bread which gives us life
and drink the cup which makes us one.

May it be the fountain
of the unfailing waters of salvation.

Here may we draw close to Christ,
the living stone,
and, in him, grow into a holy temple.

Here may our lives of holiness
become a pleasing sacrifice to your glory.

℞. Blessed be God for ever.

The bishop puts incense into some censers and incenses the altar; receiving the miter, he returns to the chair, is incensed, and then sits. Ministers, walking through the church, incense the people and the main body of the church.

22. If the altar is to be dedicated, the profession of faith is said, and the general intercessions are omitted, and what is laid down in Chapter Four, nos. 43-56, is observed.

But if the altar is to be neither blessed nor consecrated (for example, because an altar already blessed or dedicated has been transferred to the new church), after the general intercessions the Mass proceeds as in no. 23 below.

PART IV

LITURGY OF THE EUCHARIST

23. Ministers cover the altar with a cloth, and, if opportune, decorate it with flowers. They arrange in a suitable manner the candles needed for the celebration of Mass, and, if need be, the cross.

24. When the altar is ready, some of the congregation bring bread, wine, and water for the celebration of the Lord's sacrifice. The bishop receives the gifts at the chair. While the gifts are being brought, one of the following antiphons may be sung.

> If you are bringing your gift to the altar, and there you remember that your neighbor has something against you, leave your gift in front of the altar; go at once and make peace with your neighbor, and then come back and offer your gift, alleluia.

Or:

> Moses consecrated the altar to the Lord and offered sacrifices and burnt offerings; he made an evening sacrifice of sweet fragrance to the Lord God in the sight of the children of Israel.

Another appropriate song may be sung.

■ **25.** When all is ready, the bishop goes to the altar, removes the miter, and kisses the altar. The Mass proceeds in the usual way; however, neither the gifts nor the altar are incensed. But if the altar was not blessed or dedicated in this celebration, the incensation takes place in the usual way.

26. If a chapel of the blessed sacrament is to be inaugurated, when the communion of the congregation is finished, everything takes place as described in Chapter Two, nos. 79-82.

Blessing and Dismissal

■ **27.** The bishop receives the miter and says:

The Lord be with you.

R. And also with you.

Then the deacon, if appropriate, gives the invitation to the people in these or similar words:

Bow your heads and pray for God's blessing.

■ Then the bishop extends his hands over the people and blesses them, saying:

The Lord of earth and heaven
has assembled you before him this day
to bless this house of prayer.
May he fill you with the blessings of heaven.

R. Amen.

God the Father wills that all his children
scattered through the world
become one family in his Son.
May he make you his temple,
the dwelling place of his Holy Spirit.

R. Amen.

May God free you from every bond of sin,
dwell within you and give you joy.
May you live with him for ever
in the company of all his saints.

R. Amen.

The bishop takes the pastoral staff and continues:

May almighty God bless you,
the Father, and the Son, + and the Holy Spirit.

R. Amen.

28. Finally the deacon dismisses the people in the usual way.

CHAPTER SIX

RITE OF BLESSING AN ALTAR

INTRODUCTION

1.   "A fixed altar is one so constructed that it is attached to the floor so that it cannot be moved; a movable altar can be transferred from place to place."[1]

    A fixed altar is to be dedicated according to the rite described in chapter four. A movable altar also deserves religious respect because it is a table set aside solely and permanently for the eucharistic banquet. Consequently, before a movable altar is put to use, if it is not dedicated, it should at least be blessed with the following rite.[2]

2.   A movable altar may be constructed of any solid material that the traditions and culture of different regions determine to be suitable for liturgical use.[3]

3.   To erect a movable altar what is laid down in the Introduction to chapter four, nos. 6-10, is to be followed, with the necessary modifications. However, it is not permissible to place the relics of saints in the base of a movable altar.

4.   It is appropriate that a movable altar be blessed by the bishop of the diocese or by the priest who is rector of the church.

5.   A movable altar may be blessed on any day, except Good Friday and Holy Saturday. As far as possible, a day should be chosen when the people can be present in large numbers, especially a Sunday, unless pastoral considerations suggest otherwise.

6.   In the rite of blessing a movable altar the Mass is the Mass of the day.

7.   The altar should be left bare until the beginning of the liturgy of the eucharist. Hence a cross (if need be), and altar cloth, candles, and everything else necessary to prepare the altar should be on hand at a convenient place in the sanctuary.

---

[1] GIRM, no. 261.
[2] See GIRM, no. 265.
[3] See GIRM, no. 264.

OUTLINE OF THE RITE

INTRODUCTORY RITES

LITURGY OF THE WORD
    First Reading
    Responsorial Psalm
    [Second Reading]
    Gospel Acclamation
    Gospel
    Homily
    [Profession of Faith]
    General Intercessions

BLESSING OF THE ALTAR
    Invitation to Prayer
    Prayer of Blessing
    Sprinkling and Incensation of the Altar

LITURGY OF THE EUCHARIST
    Preparation of the Altar
    Presentation of the Gifts
    Eucharistic Prayer

    _____

    Communion
    Prayer after Communion

CONCLUDING RITE
    Blessing and Dismissal

RITE OF BLESSING

■ **8.** During Mass everything takes place in the usual way. When the general intercessions are finished the bishop goes to bless the altar. Meanwhile the following antiphon is sung.

> May the children of the Church be like olive branches around the table of the Lord (alleluia).

Another appropriate song may be sung.

■ **9.** When the singing is finished, the bishop, standing without miter, speaks to the people in these or similar words:

Brothers and sisters, our community rejoices as it comes together to bless this altar. Let us ask God to look kindly on the Church's offering placed upon it and to receive his people as an everlasting gift.

■ All pray in silence for a brief period. Then the bishop, with hands extended, says:

Blessed are you, Lord our God,
who accepted the sacrifice of Christ,
offered on the altar of the cross
for the salvation of the world.

Now with a Father's love,
you call your people to celebrate his memory
by coming together at his table.

May this altar,
which we have built for your holy mysteries,
be the center of our praise and thanksgiving.

May it be the table
at which we break the bread which gives us life
and drink the cup which makes us one.

May it be the fountain
of the unfailing waters of salvation.

▶

Here may we draw close to Christ,
the living stone,
and, in him, grow into a holy temple.

Here may our lives of holiness
become a pleasing sacrifice to your glory.

℞. **Blessed be God for ever.**

10. The bishop then sprinkles the altar with holy water and incenses it. Then he returns to the chair, receives the miter, is incensed, and then sits. A minister incenses the people.

11. Ministers cover the altar with a cloth, and, if opportune, decorate it with flowers; they arrange in a suitable manner the candles needed for the celebration of Mass, and, if need be, the cross.

12. When the altar is ready, some of the congregation bring bread, wine, and water for the celebration of the Lord's sacrifice. The bishop receives the gifts at the chair. While the gifts are being brought, the following antiphon may be sung.

> **If you are bringing your gift to the altar, and there you remember that your neighbor has something against you, leave your gift in front of the altar; go at once and make peace with your neighbor, and then come back and offer your gift, alleluia.**

Another appropriate song may be sung.

13. When all is ready, the bishop goes to the altar, removes the miter, and kisses the altar. The Mass proceeds in the usual way; however, neither the gifts nor the altar are incensed.

CHAPTER SEVEN

RITE OF BLESSING A CHALICE AND PATEN

INTRODUCTION

1. The chalice and paten for offering, consecrating, and receiving the bread and wine[1] have as their sole and permanent purpose the celebration of the eucharist and are therefore "sacred vessels."

2. The intention to devote these vessels entirely to the celebration of the eucharist is expressed in the presence of the community through a special blessing, which is preferably to be imparted within Mass.

3. Any priest may bless a chalice and paten, provided they have been made in conformity with the norms given in the General Instruction of the Roman Missal nos. 290-295.

4. If only a chalice or only a paten is to be blessed, the text should be modified accordingly.

---

[1]See GIRM, no. 289.

OUTLINE OF THE RITE

INTRODUCTORY RITES

LITURGY OF THE WORD
    Readings
    Homily
    General Intercessions

BLESSING OF THE CHALICE AND PATEN
    Placing of the Chalice and Paten on the Altar
    Prayer of Blessing

LITURGY OF THE EUCHARIST
    Preparation of the Altar
    Presentation of the Gifts
    Eucharistic Prayer

———————

    Communion
    Prayer after Communion

CONCLUDING RITE
    Blessing and Dismissal

RITE OF BLESSING WITHIN MASS

5. In the liturgy of the word, apart from the days listed on the Table of Liturgical Days, nos. 1-9, one or two readings may be taken from those given below in nos. 6-8.

Readings from Sacred Scripture

6. 1. 1 Corinthians 10:14-22a (Gr. 10-22) "Our blessing-cup is a communion with the blood of Christ."

2. 1 Corinthians 11:23-26 "This cup is the new covenant in my blood."

Responsorial Psalms

7. 1. Psalm 16:5 and 8, 9-10, 11
℟. (5a) The Lord is my inheritance and my cup.

2. Psalm 23:1-3a, 3b-4, 5, 6
℟. (5a, d) You prepared a banquet before me; my cup overflows.

Gospels

8. 1. Matthew 20:20-28 "You shall indeed drink my cup."

2. Mark 14:12-16, 22-26 "This is my body. This is my blood."

■ **9.** After the reading of the word of God the homily is given in which the celebrant explains the biblical readings and the meaning of the blessing of a chalice and paten that are used in the celebration of the Lord's Supper.

■ **10.** When the general intercessions are finished, ministers or representatives of the community that are presenting the chalice and paten place them on the altar. The celebrant then approaches the altar. Meanwhile the following antiphon is sung.

I will take the cup of salvation and call on the name of the Lord.

Another appropriate song may be sung.

■ **11.** When the singing is finished, the celebrant says:

Let us pray.

■   All pray in silence for a brief period. The celebrant then continues:

Lord,
with joy we place on your altar
this cup and this paten,
vessels with which we will celebrate
the sacrifice of Christ's new covenant.

May they be sanctified,
for in them the body and blood of Christ
will be offered, consecrated, and received.

Lord,
when we celebrate Christ's faultless sacrifice on earth,
may we be renewed in strength
and filled with your Spirit,
until we join with your saints
at your table in heaven.

Glory and honor be yours for ever and ever.

℟. Blessed be God for ever.

12. Afterward the ministers place a corporal on the altar. Some of the congregation bring bread, wine, and water for the celebration of the Lord's sacrifice. The celebrant puts the gifts in the newly blessed paten and chalice and offers them in the usual way. Meanwhile the following antiphon may be sung with Psalm 116:10-19.

    I will take the cup of salvation and offer a sacrifice of praise (alleluia).

    Another appropriate song may be sung.

■ **13.** When he has said the prayer **Lord God, we ask you to receive us,** the celebrant may incense the gifts and the altar.

14. If the circumstances of the celebration permit, it is appropriate that the congregation should receive the blood of Christ from the newly blessed chalice.

OUTLINE OF THE RITE

INTRODUCTORY RITES
    Greeting
    Brief Address

LITURGY OF THE WORD
    Reading(s)
    Homily

BLESSING OF THE CHALICE AND PATEN
    Placing of the Chalice and Paten on the Altar
    Prayer of Blessing
    General Intercessions
    Lord's Prayer
    Concluding Prayer

CONCLUDING RITE
    Blessing and Dismissal

RITE OF BLESSING OUTSIDE MASS

■ **15.** After the people have assembled, the celebrant, with alb or surplice and stole, goes to the chair. Meanwhile, an antiphon with Psalm 116:10-19 (see above, no. 12) may be sung or another appropriate song.

■ **16.** The celebrant greets the people saying:

The grace of our Lord Jesus Christ,
who offered for us his body and blood,
the love of God,
and the fellowship of the Holy Spirit
be with you all.

R. **And also with you.**

Other suitable words taken preferably from sacred Scripture may be used.

■ **17.** Then the celebrant briefly addresses the people, preparing them to take part in the celebration and explaining to them the meaning of the rite.

18. Afterward one or more texts from sacred Scripture are read, especially from those proposed above, with a suitable intervening responsorial psalm (see above, nos. 6-8) or a period of silence.

■ **19.** After the reading of the word of God the homily is given, in which the celebrant explains the biblical readings and the meaning of the blessing of a chalice and paten that are used in the celebration of the Lord's Supper.

■ **20.** After the homily the ministers or representatives of the community that are presenting the chalice and paten place them on the altar. The celebrant then approaches the altar. Meanwhile the following antiphon may be sung.

I will take the cup of salvation and call on the name of the Lord.

Another appropriate song may be sung.

■ **21.** Then the celebrant says:

Let us pray.

■ All pray in silence for a brief period. The celebrant then continues:

Father,
look kindly upon your children,
who have placed on your altar
this cup and this paten.

May these vessels be sanctified + by your blessing,
for with them we will celebrate
the sacrifice of Christ's new covenant.

And may we who celebrate these mysteries on earth
be renewed in strength
and filled with your Spirit
until we join with your saints
at your table in heaven.

Glory and honor be yours for ever and ever.

R. **Blessed be God for ever.**

22. Afterward the general intercessions take place either in the usual way or as indicated below:

Let us pray to the Lord Jesus who continuously offers himself for the Church, as the bread of life and the cup of salvation. With confidence we make our prayer:

Christ Jesus, bread of heaven, grant us eternal life.

Savior of all, in obedience to the Father's will, you drank the cup of suffering,
—grant that we may share in the mystery of your death and thus win the promise of eternal life.

Priest of the most high, hidden yet present in the sacrament of the altar,
—grant that we may discern by faith what is concealed from our eyes.

Good shepherd, you give yourself to your disciples as food and drink,
—grant that, fed by this mystery, we may be transformed into your likeness.

Lamb of God, you commanded your Church to celebrate the paschal mystery under the signs of bread and wine,
—grant that this memorial may be the summit and source of holiness for all who believe.

Son of God, you wondrously satisfy the hunger and thirst of all who eat and drink at your table,
—grant that through the mystery of the eucharist we may learn to live your command of love.

■ Then the celebrant may introduce the Lord's Prayer in these or similar words:

Fastened to the cross, Christ was the way of salvation; in fulfilling the will of the Father he is acclaimed the master of prayer; let his prayer be the source of ours as we say:

All:

Our Father...

■ The celebrant immediately continues:

Lord,
by the death and resurrection of your Son
you have brought redemption to the entire world.

Continue in us the work of your grace,
so that, ever recalling the mystery of Christ,
we may finally rejoice at your table in heaven.

Grant this through Christ our Lord.

R. Amen

■ 23. Then the celebrant blesses the people in the usual way and dismisses them saying:

Go in peace.

R. Thanks be to God.

APPENDIX

LITANY OF THE SAINTS

The cantors begin the litany; they add, at the proper place, names of other saints (the titular of the church, the patron saint of the place, and the saints whose relics are to be deposited, if this is to take place) and petitions suitable to the occasion.

Lord, have mercy	Lord, have mercy
Christ, have mercy	Christ, have mercy
Lord, have mercy	Lord, have mercy
Holy Mary, Mother of God	pray for us
Saint Michael	pray for us
Holy angels of God	pray for us
Saint John the Baptist	pray for us
Saint Joseph	pray for us
Saint Peter and Saint Paul	pray for us
Saint Andrew	pray for us
Saint John	pray for us
Saint Mary Magdalene	pray for us
Saint Stephen	pray for us
Saint Ignatius of Antioch	pray for us
Saint Lawrence	pray for us
Saint Perpetua and Saint Felicity	pray for us
Saint Agnes	pray for us
Saint Gregory	pray for us
Saint Augustine	pray for us
Saint Athanasius	pray for us
Saint Basil	pray for us
Saint Martin	pray for us
Saint Benedict	pray for us
Saint Francis and Saint Dominic	pray for us
Saint Francis Xavier	pray for us
Saint John Vianney	pray for us
Saint Catherine	pray for us
Saint Teresa of Jesus	pray for us
All holy men and women	pray for us

Lord, be merciful	Lord, save your people
From all evil	Lord, save your people
From every sin	Lord, save your people
From everlasting death	Lord, save your people
By your coming as man	Lord, save your people
By your death and rising to new life	Lord, save your people
By your gift of the Holy Spirit	Lord, save your people

Be merciful to us sinners	Lord, hear our prayer
Guide and protect your holy Church	Lord, hear our prayer
Keep the pope and all the clergy in faithful service to your Church	Lord, hear our prayer
Bring all peoples together in trust and peace	Lord, hear our prayer
Strengthen us in your service	Lord, hear our prayer
Make this church (altar) holy and consecrate it to your worship	Lord, hear our prayer
Jesus, Son of the living God	Lord, hear our prayer

Christ, hear us	Christ, hear us
Lord Jesus, hear our prayer	Lord Jesus, hear our prayer